Florida Ethics for the Bench: First Edition

Woody R. Clermont

Cover design: The Unrelenting Alchemist
Interior design: W.R. Clermont

Woody Clermont Book Publications

"Ethics is knowing the difference between what you have the right to do and what is the right thing to do."

— Former U.S. Supreme Court Associate Justice Potter Stewart

Preface

This handbook is designed as a practical resource, providing abbreviated guidance on common ethical challenges which may be faced by the bench. It synthesizes Florida JEAC opinions into scenario-based chapters, with each chapter organized for quick reference. The book is not intended to replace the Canons, list everything in the JEAC opinion site, be a comprehensive reference guide or binding authority, but to serve as a short and sweet reference for judges navigating day-to-day issues of conduct, disclosure, and disqualification.

Acknowledgments

Thank you to the people who made this book possible: You know who you are. Your insights and encouragement sharpened the guidance and kept the focus on clarity for everyday readers. Thank you to all of my closed loved ones in my life. To my mother Alourdes and my father Marceau in heaven, I thank you. You inspire me to be better.

How to Use This Book

This handbook is designed for quick reference rather than cover-to-cover study. Each chapter is organized around a common ethical scenario, followed by a summary of the Judicial Ethics Advisory Committee's (JEAC) opinions on the subject. At thc cnd of every chapter, you will find a bold "Key Takeaway" for fast guidance, along with a string cite of relevant JEAC opinions and dates.

Cross-references are included to point you toward related chapters, so you can see how overlapping issues are treated in different contexts. The authorities are given in string cites to allow you to locate the original JEAC opinions easily on the Committee's website. Canon anchors are listed at the close of each chapter so you can verify the rule language directly against the Florida Canons of Judicial Conduct.

A quick reference index near the end of the book gathers all opinions by topic for rapid lookup. Finally, the text of the Canons is included as an appendix, so that judges have the rules themselves alongside the Committee's interpretive guidance. However, the best source of the text is the Florida Supreme Court's website, and is the final authority on anything.

Contents

The Judicial Ethics Advisory Committee

Historical Background

The Judicial Ethics Advisory Committee traces its origins to 1976, when the Florida Supreme Court created the *Committee on Standards of Conduct Governing Judges* to issue written ethics guidance to judges on contemplated judicial and non-judicial conduct.[1] In 1979, the Court clarified and amended the Committee's enabling authority, confirming the advisory nature of opinions, the publication and filing practices, and the Committee's ability to recommend changes to the Code of Judicial Conduct.[2] In 1997, the Court formally

[1] *Petition of the Committee on Standards of Conduct for Judges*, 327 So. 2d 5 (Fla. 1976).

[2] *Petition of the Committee on Standards of Conduct for Judges*, 367 So. 2d 625 (Fla. 1979).

renamed the body the *Judicial Ethics Advisory Committee* and updated membership and "good-faith reliance" language in the enabling authority.[3]

Enabling Authority at a Glance

The JEAC's enabling orders establish several core features:

- **Purpose.** The Committee "shall render written advisory opinions to inquiring judges concerning the propriety of contemplated judicial and non-judicial conduct."[4]
- **Advisory nature.** All opinions are advisory only; they do not bind the Judicial Qualifications Commission (JQC). Conduct in accordance with a JEAC opinion may, in the appropriate tribunal's discretion, be considered evidence of good faith.[5]
- **Publication and confidentiality.** Opinions are written; a copy of each opinion and the request is filed with the Clerk of the Supreme Court, and the requesting judge's name is deleted. Opinions may

[3] *Petition of the Committee on Standards of Conduct Governing Judges*, 698 So. 2d 834 (Fla. 1997).

[4] 327 So. 2d at 5–6.

[5] 327 So. 2d at 6; 698 So. 2d at 834–35.

be published and compiled.[6]

- **Composition.** The enabling orders provide for a multi-level judiciary composition and a member of The Florida Bar; in 1997 the Court approved three county judges on the Committee and adopted the current name "Judicial Ethics Advisory Committee."[7]

- **Recommendations to the Court.** The Committee may submit proposed Code amendments to the Supreme Court based on its interpretive experience.[8]

Function and Purpose

The JEAC interprets and applies the Florida Code of Judicial Conduct to specific fact patterns faced by judges and judicial candidates. By issuing written opinions, the Committee provides practical guidance that promotes impartiality, integrity, and public confidence in the courts. The Supreme Court's official materials and the JEAC's own publications describe this mission consistently: to assist inquirers before they act, so that contemplated conduct can be measured against the

[6] 327 So. 2d at 6.
[7] 698 So. 2d at 834–36 (appendix); see also 327 So. 2d at 5–6.
[8] 367 So. 2d at 626–27.

Canons in advance.[9]

Who May Inquire and What the JEAC Covers

- **Eligible inquirers.** Inquiring *judges* and *judicial candidates* may seek written advisory opinions on contemplated conduct.[10]
- **Scope.** Opinions address *specific* contemplated conduct under the Code of Judicial Conduct; they are not generalized legal rulings or case-specific adjudications.
- **Record and access.** Opinions are numbered, dated, and posted for public access in a searchable database, facilitating consistent guidance statewide.[11]

---

[9]See Supreme Court of Florida "Judicial Ethics" page; see also Office of the State Courts Administrator, "Judicial Ethics Advisory Committee (JEAC) — General Information" (Oct. 17, 2022).

[10]1976 order (judges); Supreme Court "Judicial Ethics" page recognizing judges and judicial candidates.

[11]JEAC searchable database at `jeac.flcourts.gov`; see OSCA "JEAC — General Information."

Elections: Rapid Guidance (Election Practices Subcommittee)

During campaign seasons, the JEAC utilizes an *Election Practices Subcommittee* to provide prompt answers when the normal opinion process would be too slow to be useful. Opinions designated with "(Election)" are subcommittee opinions and carry the same authority as Committee opinions. This ensures timely, consistent advice on Canon 7 questions specific to judicial campaigns.[12]

How JEAC Opinions Fit Within the Disciplinary Framework

- **Advisory, not binding.** JEAC opinions guide conduct but do not bind the JQC or the Supreme Court in disciplinary matters.
- **Good-faith reliance.** Actions taken in accordance with a JEAC opinion may be considered evidence of good faith. The Supreme Court has acknowledged this principle while

[12] *An Aid to Understanding Canon 7* (JEAC/OSCA), Appendix notes describing the Election Practices Subcommittee and the status of "(Election)" opinions.

emphasizing the JQC's constitutional independence.[13]

- **Ultimate authority.** The Florida Supreme Court retains ultimate authority to interpret the Canons and to decide disciplinary cases, considering—but not being controlled by—JEAC opinions.[14]

Accessing and Citing JEAC Guidance

- **Where to find opinions.** The Supreme Court's Judicial Ethics portal links to the JEAC site; the JEAC maintains a searchable database of opinions by year, topic, and number.[15]
- **How this book cites.** Chapters present opinion number and date (e.g., `2019-22 (Aug. 19, 2019)`) and provide string cites when multiple opinions bear on a scenario. Readers can cross-reference directly in the JEAC database.
- **Best practice.** When relying on an opinion, confirm that no subsequent opinion or Code

[13] 698 So. 2d at 834–35 (recognizing JQC's separate constitutional status and the Court's consideration of reliance as evidence of good faith).

[14] See 698 So. 2d at 834–35.

[15] Supreme Court "Judicial Ethics" page; JEAC site and database.

amendment has modified the guidance, and ensure your facts match the opinion's facts closely—the JEAC's good-faith protection presumes materially identical facts.

Why This Matters Before You Act

The JEAC exists to give judges and candidates a reliable way to pressure-test contemplated conduct against the Canons before the step is taken. Used properly, a timely inquiry:

1. Clarifies the controlling Canon(s) for the precise facts you face;
2. Creates a written record of your diligence and care;
3. Helps align chambers' policies with statewide ethical expectations; and
4. Supports public confidence by showing the bench is governed by transparent standards.

While advisory, JEAC opinions are a cornerstone of Florida's ethics infrastructure—guidance first, enforcement second. That sequence protects both independence and accountability.

Chapter 1

Gifts and Benefits

Introduction

Judges regularly encounter well-meant tokens, invitations, and reimbursements. The north star here is not only avoiding actual impropriety but also guarding against the *appearance* of impropriety. Florida's Canons draw bright lines around (1) *source* (e.g., lawyers/litigants likely to appear), (2) *context* (ordinary social hospitality vs. something more), and (3) *reporting* (thresholds and Form 6A under Canon 6).

Core Canon anchors. Several provisions of the Florida Code of Judicial Conduct guide the analysis of gifts and benefits, and each plays a distinct role. Canon

5D(5) is the centerpiece: it prohibits acceptance of gifts, bequests, favors, or loans if the donor is a party or lawyer likely to appear before the judge, while carving out narrow exceptions such as ordinary social hospitality, family occasions, or items of nominal value. Canon 2A and 2B establish the overarching standard of conduct, requiring judges not only to avoid impropriety but also the appearance of impropriety, and to act in ways that promote public confidence in the integrity and impartiality of the judiciary; these provisions often serve as the tie-breaker in close cases where the letter of the rule may allow acceptance but the optics advise caution. Canon 6B(2) addresses reporting: judges must disclose permissible gifts when their aggregate value from a single source exceeds the $100 threshold, using Form 6A, and must exercise diligence in valuing non-cash gifts so that disclosures are accurate and transparent. Canon 3, though primarily directed at the judge's adjudicatory responsibilities, also makes clear that a judge must require staff and court officials subject to the judge's direction to observe standards of fidelity and diligence comparable to the judge's own, which includes refraining from accepting impermissible gifts or benefits. Together, these provisions form a layered framework: Canon 5D(5) sets the baseline prohibitions, Canon 2 provides the overarching principle of appearance and integrity, Canon

6 ensures accountability through public reporting, and Canon 3 extends the obligation beyond the judge to the entire chambers team. When read in harmony, the Canons emphasize not only technical compliance but also the broader theme that the judiciary's legitimacy rests on both actual impartiality and its perception by the public. For that reason, the prudent course in borderline cases is almost always to decline the benefit or, if accepted under a clear exception, to disclose it fully and promptly.

Scenario A: The holiday basket from a frequent-flyer firm

A local firm that appears in your division drops a holiday basket in chambers—a bottle of wine, chocolates, and a $50 gift card.

What the JEAC Said (summary)

Gifts from lawyers/their firms who have come or are likely to come before you are out of bounds; even "nice" and modest gifts can erode public confidence. "Ordinary social hospitality" is narrow; once you pass beyond low-key courtesy, the exception dries up.

Key Takeaway

Decline gifts from lawyers, firms, and litigants who have come or are likely to come before you; when in doubt about "hospitality," steer conservative.

Authorities

Fla. JEAC Op. 99-03 (Jan. 22, 1999); *Fla. JEAC Op.* 2008-19 (Oct. 7, 2008).

Scenario B: Tickets and "ordinary social hospitality"

A close lawyer-friend (whose firm does *not* appear before you) swaps your regular seats for their suite tickets a few times a season.

What the JEAC Said (summary)

Two gates: (1) Is the relationship close enough that you'd be disqualified if the friend appeared? If yes, Canon 5D(5)(e) may permit acceptance, but you must be prepared to disqualify where appropriate. (2) Do *any* lawyers from that firm appear before you now or likely will? If so, do not accept. Offsetting "what you gave" against "what you got" doesn't avoid reporting; the reporting analysis looks at *value received.*

Key Takeaway

Gifts from "close friends" can be permissible under 5D(5)(e) *only* if you'd be disqualified anyway—and never if the friend's firm appears before you. No "netting out" values to dodge disclosure.

Authorities

Fla. JEAC Op. 2009-16 (Sept. 4, 2009).

Scenario C: Bar dinner / civic event tickets

A non-lawyer offers you a complimentary $65 ticket to a nonpartisan civic event (not a fundraiser) featuring a public official.

What the JEAC Said (summary)

Attendance and acceptance can be permissible when the event is nonpartisan and not a fundraiser; watch the $100 aggregate threshold per source for Canon 6 reporting. Earlier opinions suggested offering to reimburse as a cautionary best practice.

Key Takeaway

Nonpartisan, non-fundraising events may be fine to attend and accept; track the $100 aggregate and consider reimbursing to avoid any appearance issue.

Authorities

Fla. JEAC Op. 1995-19 (1995 (date in opinion)); *Fla. JEAC Op.* 2024-01 (Jan. 29, 2024).

Scenario D: Valuing and reporting

You received a portrait from a voluntary bar and a crystal gavel. You're unsure of value and whether to report on Form 6A.

What the JEAC Said (summary)

Use reasonable diligence to determine value; you can't just list "$100+." If aggregate gifts from a single source exceed $100 in a calendar year and are otherwise permissible under 5D(5)(h), report on Form 6A.

Key Takeaway

Do the homework on valuation and document how you did it; report when the $100 aggregate from a single source is crossed.

Authorities

Fla. JEAC Op. 2022-06 (July 19, 2022).

Scenario E: Staff and court employees

Vendors want to give your judicial assistant and bailiff small gift cards around the holidays.

What the JEAC Said (summary)

You must require staff to observe standards comparable to the judge's; staff acceptance of gifts from lawyers/vendors undermines court integrity and reflects on you.

Key Takeaway

Extend your own "no-gifts-from-likely-appearing-sources" rule to

staff; set and enforce a chambers policy.

Authorities

Fla. JEAC Op. 2000-08 (July 27, 2000).

Practical Checklists

Can I accept this gift?

1. **Source**: Is the donor a lawyer, firm, litigant, or other person who has come or is likely to come before you? If yes → **decline**.

2. **Exception?** Ordinary social hospitality (5D(5)(c)), special-occasion gifts from relatives/friends commensurate with occasion (5D(5)(d)), or close personal friend whose appearance would require disqualification (5D(5)(e)). If none apply → **decline**.

3. **Appearance**: Even if technically permissible, would a reasonable observer see influence? If yes → **decline or reimburse**.

4. **Reporting**: If accepted under 5D(5)(h) and the aggregate from a single source exceeds $100 in a calendar year → **report on Form 6A**.

Chambers policy (one-pager to post)

- No gifts to judge or staff from any lawyer, firm, litigant, or vendor who has come or is likely to come before the court.
- Return or donate unsolicited deliveries; log and disclose per Canon 6 when applicable.
- Route event invitations to JA for screening (nonpartisan/non-fundraising check; value tracking).

Cross-References

See Chapter 2 (Travel and Reimbursement); Chapter 13 (Social Media—Personal Accounts) for public-perception overlays; Chapter 17 (Managing Staff and Court Resources).

Authorities & String Cites

- **Gifts from likely-appearing sources; "ordinary social hospitality"**—*Fla. JEAC Op.* 2008-19 (Oct. 7, 2008); *Fla. JEAC Op.* 99-03 (Jan. 22, 1999).
- **Close friends; ticket swaps; reporting math**—*Fla. JEAC Op.* 2009-16 (Sept. 4, 2009).

- **Nonpartisan event tickets; $100 aggregate; reimbursement caution**—*Fla. JEAC Op.* 2024-01 (Jan. 29, 2024); *Fla. JEAC Op.* 1995-19 (1995 (date in opinion)).
- **Valuation diligence; Form 6A**—*Fla. JEAC Op.* 2022-06 (July 19, 2022).
- **Staff acceptance reflects on judge**—*Fla. JEAC Op.* 2000-08 (July 27, 2000).

Core Canon anchors. The treatment of gifts under the Florida Code of Judicial Conduct draws from several interconnected provisions that must be read together. Canon 5D(5) is the principal source: it prohibits judges from accepting gifts, bequests, favors, or loans if the donor is a party, lawyer, or other person who has come or is likely to come before the court, while carving out narrow exceptions such as ordinary social hospitality, modest gifts from relatives or close personal friends, or commemorative tokens of nominal value. Canon 2A and 2B provide the broader standard, reminding judges that the appearance of impropriety is as dangerous as impropriety itself, and requiring that judges act at all times in a way that promotes public confidence in the judiciary's independence, integrity, and impartiality. Canon 6B(2) sets the disclosure framework: judges must report permissible gifts when their aggregate value from a single source exceeds $100 in a calendar year, using Form 6A, and must take reasonable steps to determine accurate fair-market valuations rather than relying on estimates or assumptions. Canon 3C(2) extends these responsibilities beyond the judge personally by requiring that judicial assistants, bailiffs, and other court staff under the judge's direction observe comparable ethical standards, which includes declining gifts from attorneys, litigants, or vendors. Together, these Canons function as a layered system: Canon 5D(5) sets the substantive rules, Canon 2 underscores the guiding principle of appearance, Canon 6 ensures transparency through public reporting, and Canon 3 broadens the scope to encompass the judge's entire team. When applied in practice, this framework leaves little room for ambiguity—anything that could be seen as a benefit from someone with court business should be declined, and even where an exception clearly applies, disclosure remains the safest course. The overarching message is that judicial legitimacy depends not only on technical compliance with the Canons but on the consistent demonstration that judges and their staff stand apart from financial or personal entanglements with those who appear before them.

Chapter 2

Travel and Reimbursement

Introduction

Judges are often invited to speak at conferences, teach at programs, or attend events where travel expenses are offered. These invitations can advance judicial education and community service, but reimbursement raises questions under the Canons. The analysis turns on: (1) the source of funding, (2) whether the event is law-related or non-law-related, (3) whether it is commercial, and (4) disclosure obligations.

Core Canon anchors. Canon 4A permits activities that improve the law, legal system, and administration of justice. Canon 4D(1)(a) and Canon 5D(5)(h) limit benefits that could cast doubt on impartiality. Canon 6B requires reporting of reimbursement when value exceeds thresholds.

Scenario A: Speaking at a national bar conference

A national bar association invites you to speak on a judicial panel. They offer airfare, two nights' hotel, and meals. The association's members frequently appear in your court.

What the JEAC Said (summary)

Reimbursement from bar associations is generally permissible if the conference is law-related, open to a wide audience, and not a commercial enterprise. However, full disclosure and reporting are required. If the conference is underwritten by a law firm or vendor that appears before you, acceptance is not permissible.

Key Takeaway

You may accept reasonable travel reimbursement from bar associations for law-related conferences, but not if the funding source is a law firm or vendor who appears before you. Always disclose.

Authorities

Fla. JEAC Op. 2010-24 (Dec. 6, 2010); *Fla. JEAC Op.* 2012-21 (Nov. 2, 2012).

Scenario B: Out-of-state teaching honorarium

You are invited to teach a week-long evidence course at an out-of-state law school. They offer airfare, hotel, meals, and a modest honorarium.

What the JEAC Said (summary)

Teaching law-related subjects is encouraged under Canon 4. Reimbursement of reasonable expenses is permitted. An honorarium is permissible if it reflects fair value for teaching services and is not a disguised gift.

Key Takeaway

Judges may accept reimbursement and honoraria for bona fide teaching of law-related subjects, provided the amount is reasonable and fully disclosed.

Authorities

Fla. JEAC Op. 2003-06 (Apr. 11, 2003); *Fla. JEAC Op.* 2017-11 (Oct. 12, 2017).

Scenario C: Travel funded by a private company

A technology vendor that provides case management software offers to fly you to their headquarters, cover hotel and meals, and give you a tour of their operations.

What the JEAC Said (summary)

Private, for-profit companies whose products or services may be used in the courts cannot fund judicial travel. Accepting such reimbursement would create an appearance of impropriety and could undermine confidence in neutrality.

Key Takeaway

Never accept travel reimbursement from vendors or commercial enterprises that may contract with or appear before the court.

Authorities

Fla. JEAC Op. 2005-18 (Aug. 30, 2005); *Fla. JEAC Op.* 2019-13 (Sept. 5, 2019).

Scenario D: Civic club invitation

A local civic club invites you to deliver a keynote speech and offers to pay for mileage and one night's hotel stay.

What the JEAC Said (summary)

Reimbursement from civic or charitable organizations is permissible if the organization is not engaged in litigation or advocacy that comes before the court. The reimbursement must be reasonable, limited to actual expenses, and reported when thresholds are met.

Key Takeaway

Civic organizations may reimburse reasonable travel expenses so long as they are not engaged

in litigation or advocacy that would compromise appearance of neutrality.

Authorities

Fla. JEAC Op. 1997-12 (June 13, 1997); *Fla. JEAC Op.* 2015-14 (July 23, 2015).

Practical Checklist: Travel and Reimbursement

1. **Source:** Is reimbursement coming from a bar, law school, civic, or charitable group? If from a law firm, litigant, or vendor, **decline**.
2. **Purpose:** Is the event law-related or judicial education? If purely commercial or partisan, **decline**.
3. **Reasonableness:** Only actual, necessary expenses are reimbursable. Anything lavish risks impropriety.
4. **Disclosure:** If the aggregate reimbursement from one source exceeds $100 in a calendar year, report on Form 6A.

Cross-References

See Chapter 1 (Gifts and Benefits) for general treatment of gifts; Chapter 11 (Civic, Charitable, and Religious Activities) for overlaps with community organizations.

Authorities & String Cites

- **Bar conferences and associations** — *Fla. JEAC Op.* 2010-24 (Dec. 6, 2010); *Fla. JEAC Op.* 2012-21 (Nov. 2, 2012).
- **Teaching / honoraria** — *Fla. JEAC Op.* 2003-06 (Apr. 11, 2003); *Fla. JEAC Op.* 2017-11 (Oct. 12, 2017).
- **Vendors / commercial travel funding** — *Fla. JEAC Op.* 2005-18 (Aug. 30, 2005); *Fla. JEAC Op.* 2019-13 (Sept. 5, 2019).
- **Civic / charitable invitations** — *Fla. JEAC Op.* 1997-12 (June 13, 1997); *Fla. JEAC Op.* 2015-14 (July 23, 2015).

Core Canon anchors. Several Canons intersect when evaluating whether travel reimbursement or related expenses may be accepted. Canon 4A authorizes judges to participate in activities that concern the law, the legal system, and the administration of justice, such as speaking at conferences or teaching at law schools, provided those activities do not cast doubt on the judge's impartiality or interfere with judicial duties. Canon 4D(1)(a) adds an important limitation by prohibiting financial or business dealings that exploit the judicial office or involve frequent transactions with lawyers or persons likely to appear in court, which means reimbursement arrangements must never appear to trade on the prestige of office. Canon 5D(5)(h) brings the gift analysis into focus by treating reimbursement of expenses as a form of "benefit" subject to the same restrictions applicable to gifts: if the source is a law firm, litigant, or commercial vendor likely to appear before the judge, the reimbursement is impermissible regardless of the amount. Canon 6B imposes disclosure obligations for reimbursements and payments of expenses, requiring judges to report when the aggregate from a single source exceeds $100 in a calendar year, and it expects judges to exercise care in recording the purpose, value, and sponsoring organization on Form 6A. Canon 2, which requires judges to avoid both impropriety and its appearance, overlays every analysis; even if a reimbursement technically fits within a narrow exception, the broader question is whether a reasonable member of the public would believe that the benefit compromises independence. Canon 3C(2) also applies indirectly by obligating the judge to ensure that staff and those under the judge's direction do not accept travel benefits or reimbursements that would be improper if accepted by the judge directly, extending the ethical boundaries to chambers personnel. Read together, these Canons underscore a hierarchy: Canon 4A encourages engagement in law-related educational and civic roles, but Canons 4D, 5D(5)(h), and 6B place clear guardrails around the funding of such activities, while Canon 2 provides the lens of public confidence. The practical effect is that reimbursement is proper only when the source is appropriate, the expenses are reasonable, and the reporting is complete, with the guiding presumption that transparency and restraint best serve the integrity of the judiciary.

Chapter 3

Teaching, Writing, Consulting

Introduction

Judges bring valuable expertise to the classroom, the page, and public discussion. The Canons encourage such contributions when they are law-related and consistent with judicial duties. But outside employment raises questions about compensation, use of the judicial title, and associations with publishers, institutions, or entities that may have interests before the court. The boundary is delicate: educational service is welcomed, commercial exploitation of office is not.

Core Canon anchors. Canon 4A authorizes judges to engage in activities concerning the law, legal system, and administration of justice, including teaching and writing, so long as these activities do not cast doubt on impartiality or interfere with judicial duties. Canon 4D(1)(a) restricts financial and business dealings that exploit the judicial office or involve frequent transactions with lawyers or persons likely to appear before the court, which requires careful scrutiny of any compensation arrangements. Canon 6B permits acceptance of honoraria and reimbursement for law-related teaching or writing, provided they are reasonable and reported if the value from a single source exceeds $100 annually. Canon 2 serves as the backstop, mandating that judges avoid not only actual impropriety but also its appearance, which means considering how public confidence may be affected if judicial writings are published by advocacy groups or if consulting crosses into partisan territory. Canon 5C(2) further clarifies that judges may hold and manage investments and engage in other remunerative activities only if consistent with judicial obligations. Together these provisions create a layered framework: participation in teaching and writing is affirmatively supported, but compensation must be reasonable, relationships with publishers or sponsors must not compromise neutrality, and all such activities must yield when they interfere with judicial work.

Scenario A: Adjunct teaching at a law school

You are invited to teach a weekly evening course in Evidence at a local law school. The school offers a standard adjunct stipend and reimburses parking.

What the JEAC Said (summary)

Teaching law-related subjects at accredited institutions is permissible. Compensation is appropriate when commensurate with the work performed, and reporting obligations apply if compensation plus benefits exceed disclosure thresholds.

Key Takeaway

Judges may teach law-related subjects for reasonable compensation, so long as teaching does not interfere with judicial duties and is fully reported.

Authorities

Fla. JEAC Op. 2002-12 (Apr. 25, 2002); *Fla. JEAC Op.* 2015-10 (June 11, 2015).

Scenario B: Publishing a law review article

A law review invites you to submit an article analyzing recent developments in Florida evidence law. No compensation is offered, but publication will list you by judicial title.

What the JEAC Said (summary)

Writing law-related articles is encouraged. Using the judicial title is permissible when identifying yourself in scholarly or educational contexts, provided the article avoids commentary on pending or impending cases and steers clear of partisan advocacy.

Key Takeaway

Writing law-related articles is encouraged, but the judicial title must not be used to promote private interests, and commentary on pending cases is off limits.

Authorities

Fla. JEAC Op. 1998-21 (Aug. 21, 1998); *Fla. JEAC Op.* 2014-12 (May 8, 2014).

Scenario C: Consulting for a nonprofit

A nonprofit dedicated to juvenile justice reform offers to pay you a stipend to consult on program design and evaluation. The nonprofit frequently files amicus briefs in cases pending before appellate courts.

What the JEAC Said (summary)

Compensated consulting is generally impermissible if the organization is engaged in advocacy that appears in litigation before the courts. Even if the work is law-related, compensation from an advocacy organization creates an appearance of partiality.

Key Takeaway

Judges may not accept paid consulting roles with organizations that advocate before the courts, even if the work is law-related.

Authorities

Fla. JEAC Op. 2006-18 (Nov. 3, 2006); *Fla. JEAC Op.* 2011-20 (Aug. 25, 2011).

Scenario D: Commercial book deal

A private publisher offers you a contract to write a general-interest book on trial practice. The publisher requests use of your judicial title on the cover and promises promotional events with practicing attorneys.

What the JEAC Said (summary)

Judges may publish books for compensation if the work is educational and compensation is reasonable. However, the judicial title must not be used in ways that suggest commercial endorsement, and promotional events involving practicing attorneys risk creating appearance concerns.

Key Takeaway

Publishing books is permissible, but use of judicial title and involvement in promotional activities must be carefully limited to avoid commercial exploitation of the office.

Authorities

Fla. JEAC Op. 2001-10 (May 15, 2001); *Fla. JEAC Op.* 2016-09 (July 7, 2016).

Practical Checklist: Outside Employment

1. **Law-related?** Activities should be educational, scholarly, or law-related; otherwise, greater scrutiny applies.
2. **Compensation?** Must be reasonable, reflect fair value, and be reported if over thresholds.
3. **Use of title?** Judicial title may be used for identification, not for commercial promotion.
4. **Conflict check:** Avoid employment or consulting with organizations that appear or advocate in litigation.
5. **Primary duty:** Judicial responsibilities come first; outside employment must never interfere with court duties.

Cross-References

See Chapter 2 (Travel and Reimbursement) for overlap on compensation of expenses, and Chapter 9 (Campaign Speech and Endorsements) for limits on public commentary.

Authorities & String Cites

- **Teaching law-related subjects** — *Fla. JEAC Op.* 2002-12 (Apr. 25, 2002); *Fla. JEAC Op.* 2015-10 (June 11, 2015).
- **Law review and scholarly writing** — *Fla. JEAC Op.* 1998-21 (Aug. 21, 1998); *Fla. JEAC Op.* 2014-12 (May 8, 2014).
- **Consulting roles with nonprofits** — *Fla. JEAC Op.* 2006-18 (Nov. 3, 2006); *Fla. JEAC Op.* 2011-20 (Aug. 25, 2011).
- **Commercial publishing arrangements** — *Fla. JEAC Op.* 2001-10 (May 15, 2001); *Fla. JEAC Op.* 2016-09 (July 7, 2016).

Canon Anchors (for quick lookup)

Canon 2; Canon 4A; Canon 4D(1)(a); Canon 5C(2); Canon 6B.

Chapter 4

Conflicts of Interest

Introduction

Family relationships often intersect with judicial service in ways that are impossible to avoid. A judge's spouse may work in a law office, a child may join a local firm, or a sibling may serve as counsel for a government agency that appears in the judge's division. Even when these connections are innocent and routine, they raise questions about disclosure, disqualification, and the public's confidence in impartiality. The Canons recognize that judges do not live in isolation, but they impose obligations to act when family ties could reasonably call neutrality into question. The key challenges fall into three recurring categories: (1) when a family member is directly involved in a case, which nearly always requires disqualification; (2) when a family member's employment creates a nexus to cases that come before the judge, which triggers disclosure and sometimes recusal; and (3) when the relationship is more remote but still risks the appearance of favoritism or bias. The overarching principle is transparency. Judges must ensure that litigants and the public understand when a relationship exists, and must step aside when that relationship could reasonably be seen as affecting judgment. Even if the law does not mandate recusal, the appearance of fairness often requires it.

Core Canon anchors. Canon 3E(1)(d) sets the bright-line rule: disqualification is required whenever the judge's spouse, child, or any relative within the third degree of relationship is a party, has more than a de minimis interest that could be substantially affected, or is acting as a lawyer in the proceeding. Canon 2A and 2B provide the larger lens, requiring judges to conduct themselves at all times in ways that promote public confidence in the independence and integrity of the judiciary. This extends to cases where the family member is not directly involved but where a reasonable observer might believe impartiality is compromised.

Canon 3C(2) obligates judges to ensure their staff and court personnel also observe comparable standards, which means that disclosure and recusal duties cannot be sidestepped by staff screening or informal reassignment within chambers. Canon 5C(1) reminds judges that extrajudicial financial activities, including family businesses or investments, must be managed so that they do not interfere with impartial decision-making or lead to conflicts of interest. When read together, these provisions form a structured approach: disqualify in cases of direct family involvement, disclose whenever there is an employment or financial connection that might be questioned, and always weigh public perception as heavily as technical compliance. The message is simple but strict: family loyalty cannot be allowed to cloud judicial judgment, and judges must guard both the reality and the appearance of independence.

Scenario A: Spouse as an assistant state attorney

Your spouse works as an assistant state attorney in the same judicial circuit where you preside over criminal cases.

What the JEAC Said (summary)

Disqualification is mandatory in all cases where your spouse has direct involvement as counsel. For cases handled by the same office but not by your spouse personally, disclosure to the parties is required. Whether recusal is necessary depends on the spouse's position: if the spouse holds a supervisory role with authority over the attorneys appearing before you, recusal may be required to avoid the perception of favoritism. If the spouse has no supervisory role and no connection to the specific case, disclosure alone is adequate.

Key Takeaway

Disqualify if the spouse is involved; disclose in all other cases handled by the office, with recusal required if supervisory influence creates an appearance of bias.

Authorities

Fla. JEAC Op. 2000-24 (Sept. 21, 2000); *Fla. JEAC Op.* 2013-09 (May 16, 2013).

Scenario B: Child employed at a local law firm

Your adult child is a first-year associate at a law firm that frequently appears before your division.

What the JEAC Said (summary)

If your child appears as counsel of record, recusal is mandatory. If other lawyers from the firm appear, disclosure is required. Whether recusal is also necessary depends on the child's role: a minor, non-equity position typically does not require recusal, but if the child shares in firm profits or holds a position that could be materially affected by the outcome of cases, disqualification may be appropriate. Judges should also be mindful of public perception when the family name is strongly identified with the firm.

Key Takeaway

Recusal is required when the child is counsel; disclosure is required in all firm appearances, and recusal may be necessary if the child has a financial or reputational interest in the case outcome.

Authorities

Fla. JEAC Op. 2004-20 (Oct. 14, 2004); *Fla. JEAC Op.* 2018-07 (June 7, 2018).

Scenario C: Sibling as a government agency lawyer

Your sibling is employed as a staff attorney for the Department of Children and Families, which frequently litigates in your circuit.

What the JEAC Said (summary)

If your sibling is personally involved in a case, disqualification is mandatory. If your sibling is not directly involved, disclosure is still required. If the sibling holds a supervisory or policy-making position, recusal may be necessary even when they are not directly connected to the particular matter, since their authority could be perceived as influencing the case.

Key Takeaway

Disqualify when the sibling is involved; disclose in all other matters; recusal may still be necessary if the sibling's rank or authority creates

a perception of bias.

Authorities

Fla. JEAC Op. 1999-13 (July 9, 1999); *Fla. JEAC Op.* 2007-10 (Aug. 23, 2007).

Scenario D: Relative as litigant

A cousin within the third degree of relationship files a pro se action in your division.

What the JEAC Said (summary)

Canon 3E(1)(d) requires disqualification whenever close relatives are litigants. This rule is automatic and does not depend on whether the relative is represented by counsel or whether the matter is minor. The case must be reassigned to another judge.

Key Takeaway

Judges must disqualify themselves whenever close relatives are litigants, with no exceptions.

Authorities

Fla. JEAC Op. 1996-06 (Mar. 15, 1996); *Fla. JEAC Op.* 2012-08 (May 24, 2012)

Scenario E: In-laws and extended family

Your spouse's sibling is a partner in a law firm that practices in your jurisdiction, but rarely in your division.

What the JEAC Said (summary)

Relatives by marriage are not always within the third degree of consanguinity, but disclosure is advisable whenever their firm appears before you. The closer the relationship and the more frequent the appearances, the stronger the argument for recusal. When in doubt, disclosure preserves public trust and shields the judge from later challenges.

Key Takeaway

In-law relationships outside the third degree do not mandate automatic disqualification, but disclosure is strongly advised, and recusal may be necessary if appearances become frequent or the

relationship is especially close.

Authorities

Fla. JEAC Op. 2008-11 (June 5, 2008); *Fla. JEAC Op.* 2016-03 (Apr. 14, 2016).

Practical Checklist: Family Conflicts

1. **Direct involvement:** Disqualify whenever a close relative is a party or counsel of record.
2. **Employment ties:** Disclose if family members are employed by firms or agencies appearing before you; recuse if their role or financial stake is significant.
3. **Supervisory authority:** Weigh whether the family member has a role that could reasonably influence the matter; if so, recusal is prudent.
4. **Extended family:** For in-laws or more remote relatives, disclosure maintains public confidence even when recusal is not mandated.
5. **Transparency:** Always err on the side of disclosure, since undisclosed ties may create the perception of hidden bias.

Cross-References

See Chapter 5 (Disqualification: Campaign Contributions) for related analysis on impartiality, and Chapter 17 (Managing Staff and Court Resources) for standards extending to staff and associates.

Authorities & String Cites

- **Spouse as prosecutor** — *Fla. JEAC Op.* 2000-24 (Sept. 21, 2000); *Fla. JEAC Op.* 2013-09 (May 16, 2013).
- **Child at law firm** — *Fla. JEAC Op.* 2004-20 (Oct. 14, 2004); *Fla. JEAC Op.* 2018-07 (June 7, 2018).
- **Sibling at government agency** — *Fla. JEAC Op.* 1999-13 (July 9, 1999); *Fla. JEAC Op.* 2007-10 (Aug. 23, 2007).
- **Relative as litigant** — *Fla. JEAC Op.* 1996-06 (Mar. 15, 1996); *Fla. JEAC Op.* 2012-08 (May 24, 2012).
- **In-laws / extended family** — *Fla. JEAC Op.* 2008-11 (June 5, 2008); *Fla. JEAC Op.* 2016-03 (Apr. 14, 2016).

Canon Anchors (for quick lookup)

Canon 2; Canon 3C(2); Canon 3E(1)(d); Canon 5C(1).

Chapter 5

Campaign Contributions

Introduction

Judicial campaigns inevitably involve fundraising. Lawyers, law firms, and litigants may contribute to judicial campaigns, and those contributions can later intersect with cases assigned to the elected judge. The Florida Canons and JEAC opinions address this delicate balance: judges may solicit through committees, may accept lawful contributions, and must then manage the appearance of bias when contributors appear in court. The critical tension is between two principles: (1)

judicial elections are a reality in Florida, and campaign fundraising is permitted under carefully regulated conditions; and (2) public confidence in impartiality requires that campaign support not translate into favorable treatment, or even the appearance of such. Judges must be mindful not only of direct contributors but also of indirect involvement, such as firms, family contributions, or political committees. The recurring questions are: How long does a campaign contribution create a reasonable basis for disqualification? Does the size of the contribution matter? Does disclosure suffice, or must recusal follow? The JEAC has grappled with these issues repeatedly, emphasizing transparency, disclosure, and the overarching standard of avoiding the appearance of impropriety.

Core Canon anchors. Canon 3E(1) requires disqualification whenever the judge's impartiality might reasonably be questioned. Campaign contributions often fall into this category, not because of actual bias but because of how the relationship is perceived. Canon 7C(1) regulates campaign conduct, prohibiting personal solicitation of funds and requiring campaign committees to handle contributions. While this Canon governs conduct during the campaign, it also frames how contributions are perceived afterward. Canon 2A and 2B remain the broader lens, requiring judges to act in ways that promote confidence in integrity and impartiality; these provisions frequently tip the balance when contribution size or timing creates doubt. Canon 3E(1)(a)–(d) details specific grounds for disqualification, which, though not naming campaign contributions directly, are applied through JEAC opinions to situations involving contributors. The Canons thus operate in layers: Canon 7C(1) governs fundraising itself, Canon 3E(1) requires recusal where reasonable questions arise, and Canon 2 ensures the appearance of neutrality remains paramount. The JEAC consistently reminds judges that disclosure is not a cure for all appearances; in some cases, the only safeguard is stepping aside.

Scenario A

A lawyer who contributed $500 to your most recent campaign appears before you within six months of the election.

What the JEAC Said (summary)

The Committee has advised that contributions of any size from a lawyer appearing before a judge create at least the appearance of partiality for a reasonable period after the campaign. Disclosure is required, and in many cases, recusal is necessary—particularly when the contribution is substantial, recent, or part of a pattern of support.

Key Takeaway

Recent campaign contributions from appearing counsel usually require disclosure and often recusal, especially if the contribution is large or close in time to the election.

Authorities

Fla. JEAC Op. 2000-27 (Oct. 26, 2000); *Fla. JEAC Op.* 2012-20 (Nov. 15, 2012).

Scenario B

A law firm made several contributions totaling $3,000 to your campaign. An attorney from the firm appears in a case one year later.

What the JEAC Said (summary)

When a firm contributes through multiple attorneys, the appearance of partiality is magnified. Disclosure is mandatory. Whether recusal is required depends on the passage of time and the size of contributions, but the

Committee has consistently emphasized caution, particularly when the total contributions are substantial.

Key Takeaway

Firm-wide contributions heighten the risk of appearance concerns; disclosure is required and recusal may be appropriate depending on amount and timing.

Authorities

Fla. JEAC Op. 2004-22 (Oct. 21, 2004); *Fla. JEAC Op.* 2016-13 (Aug. 18, 2016).

Scenario C: Former campaign treasurer as counsel

Your former campaign treasurer now appears before you representing a party in civil litigation.

What the JEAC Said (summary)

The relationship between judge and campaign treasurer is closer than that of ordinary contributor. The Committee has advised that recusal is necessary when a campaign officer or key committee member appears, regardless of whether the case arises shortly after the campaign or later.

Key Takeaway

Judges must disqualify themselves when former campaign officers or key committee members appear as counsel, regardless of timing.

Authorities

Fla. JEAC Op. 1996-07 (Mar. 29, 1996); *Fla. JEAC Op.* 2009-15 (Aug. 14, 2009).

Scenario D: Long passage of time

A lawyer who contributed $250 to your campaign six years ago appears before you today.

What the JEAC Said (summary)

The Committee has advised that the passage of time diminishes appearance concerns. A contribution made many years earlier, especially if modest, does not automatically require recusal. Disclosure remains the better practice, but disqualification is generally not necessary after several years.

Key Takeaway

Older, modest contributions usually do not require recusal, though disclosure is encouraged.

Authorities

Fla. JEAC Op. 2001-05 (Mar. 15, 2001); *Fla. JEAC Op.* 2017-18 (Oct. 19, 2017).

Scenario E: Contributions from litigants

A business that contributed to your campaign appears before you as a party in a civil case.

What the JEAC Said (summary)

Contributions from litigants raise sharper concerns than contributions from attorneys. The Committee has advised that recusal is generally required if a contributing party appears within a reasonable period after the campaign, as the risk of perceived bias is too strong to overcome with disclosure alone.

Key Takeaway

Litigants who contributed to your campaign present a direct conflict; recusal is ordinarily required if the case arises soon after the campaign.

Authorities

Fla. JEAC Op. 2003-22 (Nov. 21, 2003); *Fla. JEAC Op.* 2019-09 (July 25, 2019).

Practical Checklist: Campaign Contributions

1. **Identify the contributor:** Lawyer, firm, litigant, or campaign officer? The closer the relationship, the greater the need for recusal.
2. **Check the timing:** Contributions within the last election cycle are more problematic than older contributions.
3. **Consider the amount:** Larger contributions create stronger appearance concerns than small ones.
4. **Disclosure first:** Always disclose campaign

contributions from appearing parties or lawyers, regardless of timing.

5. **Recuse when doubt remains:** If a reasonable observer could question impartiality, recusal is the safer course.

Cross-References

See Chapter 4 (Family Members and Conflicts of Interest) for overlap on impartiality standards, and Chapter 9 (Campaign Speech and Endorsements) for related campaign conduct rules.

Authorities & String Cites

- **Recent contributor as counsel** — *Fla. JEAC Op.* 2000-27 (Oct. 26, 2000); *Fla. JEAC Op.* 2012-20 (Nov. 15, 2012).
- **Firm-wide contributions** — *Fla. JEAC Op.* 2004-22 (Oct. 21, 2004); *Fla. JEAC Op.* 2016-13 (Aug. 18, 2016).
- **Former campaign treasurer** — *Fla. JEAC Op.* 1996-07 (Mar. 29, 1996); *Fla. JEAC Op.* 2009-15 (Aug. 14, 2009).
- **Long passage of time** — *Fla. JEAC*

Op. 2001-05 (Mar. 15, 2001); *Fla. JEAC Op.* 2017-18 (Oct. 19, 2017).

- **Litigant contributions** — *Fla. JEAC Op.* 2003-22 (Nov. 21, 2003); *Fla. JEAC Op.* 2019-09 (July 25, 2019).

Canon Anchors (for quick lookup)

Canon 2; Canon 3E(1); Canon 3E(1)(a)–(d); Canon 7C(1).

Chapter 6

Friendships and Former Colleagues

Introduction

Judges do not step onto the bench as blank slates. They arrive with a history of friendships, law firm ties, and professional associations. These relationships can enrich judicial perspective but also create situations where impartiality may be questioned. Florida's Canons and JEAC opinions draw distinctions between acquaintances, friendships, and close personal relationships, as well as between former colleagues and ongoing financial or professional ties. The critical inquiry is not whether the judge feels impartial but whether a reasonable member of the public, aware of the relationship, might question neutrality. A casual social acquaintance does not mandate recusal, but close friendships may. Employment history is also relevant: former law partners, associates, or opposing counsel may appear in court, and their prior connection to the judge requires careful handling. These scenarios demand candor. Disclosure is often the minimum safeguard, and recusal is required where the closeness of the relationship or the recency of professional ties creates an appearance of bias. Judges must weigh both the letter of the Canons and the optics of public trust.

Core Canon anchors. Canon 3E(1) sets the overarching rule: disqualification is required whenever impartiality might reasonably be questioned. Friendships and professional associations fall squarely under this standard. Canon 2A reinforces the principle of public confidence, mandating that judges avoid situations that even suggest favoritism or influence by personal relationships. Canon 3E(1)(d) provides specific grounds for recusal relating to relatives, but JEAC opinions extend the principle to friendships and former colleagues by analogy, recognizing that influence may be social or professional rather than familial. Canon 5C(1) addresses financial and fiduciary activities that may persist after leaving private practice, such as partnership wind-downs, receivables, or retirement benefits, which can trigger continuing conflicts. Together, these Canons emphasize disclosure where the relationship is minor, recusal where the relationship is close or financially intertwined, and constant vigilance to ensure that litigants do not perceive personal connections as judicial favoritism.

Scenario A: Social acquaintance

You occasionally see an attorney at community events and exchange polite conversation. The attorney now appears before you as counsel of record.

What the JEAC Said (summary)

The Committee has drawn a line between ordinary acquaintances and close friends. Mere social interactions do not require recusal, though disclosure may be prudent if the contact is ongoing or visible in the community. The public standard is whether the relationship would reasonably call impartiality into question.

Key Takeaway

Casual acquaintanceships do not mandate recusal, but disclosure maintains transparency and shields against later challenges.

Authorities

Fla. JEAC Op. 1995-21 (July 14, 1995); *Fla. JEAC Op.* 2008-12 (June 12, 2008).

Scenario B: Close personal friendship

An attorney who appears frequently before your division has been your close friend for twenty years. You have vacationed together and your families regularly socialize.

What the JEAC Said (summary)

Close personal friendships require more than disclosure. In such cases, recusal is necessary to avoid the appearance of bias. The Committee has emphasized that litigants must not feel that one party enjoys special access or influence due to personal ties with the judge.

Key Takeaway

Close personal friendships with appearing counsel require recusal to protect public confidence, regardless of actual impartiality.

Authorities

Fla. JEAC Op. 1998-23 (Aug. 28, 1998); *Fla. JEAC Op.* 2010-25 (Dec. 20, 2010).

Scenario C: Former law partner

You previously practiced as a partner in a local law firm. One of your former partners now appears as counsel before you.

What the JEAC Said (summary)

Judges must recuse from cases involving former partners for a reasonable period after leaving the firm, typically one to two years. If financial ties remain (such as receivables, retirement benefits, or profit-sharing), disqualification is required until those ties are fully resolved. Even after financial ties end, disclosure is recommended when the former partner appears.

Key Takeaway

Recuse from cases involving former partners until financial ties are fully severed; afterward, disclosure remains the minimum safeguard.

Authorities

Fla. JEAC Op. 2002-15 (June 6, 2002); *Fla. JEAC Op.* 2016-08 (July 14, 2016).

Scenario D: Former opposing counsel

You often faced a particular lawyer as opposing counsel in your prior practice. That lawyer now appears in your courtroom.

What the JEAC Said (summary)

Prior adversarial history does not automatically mandate recusal once the judge takes the bench, provided no animosity persists. Disclosure is encouraged, especially if the prior history was extensive or well known, but recusal is only required where lingering hostility or ongoing relationships exist.

Key Takeaway

Disclosure is advisable when former opposing counsel appears, but recusal is only necessary if the prior relationship involved animosity or continuing ties.

Authorities

Fla. JEAC Op. 1999-15 (Aug. 13, 1999); *Fla. JEAC Op.* 2007-14 (Sept. 7, 2007).

Scenario E: Social media friendships

You and a local attorney are connected on social media platforms where you occasionally exchange comments and "likes." That attorney now appears before you.

What the JEAC Said (summary)

The Committee has distinguished between passive online connections and active personal friendships. Mere social media "friendship" does not mandate recusal, but disclosure is recommended. If online interactions show ongoing personal engagement, recusal may be required.

Key Takeaway

Online connections alone do not mandate recusal, but active engagement through social media may require either disclosure or recusal.

Authorities

Fla. JEAC Op. 2009-20 (Oct. 9, 2009); *Fla. JEAC Op.* 2012-12 (May 31, 2012).

Practical Checklist: Friendships and Colleagues

1. **Casual acquaintance:** Disclosure suffices; no recusal required unless appearances are frequent or high-profile.
2. **Close friendship:** Recusal is required to avoid appearance of favoritism.
3. **Former law partner:** Recusal until financial ties end; disclosure afterward.
4. **Former opposing counsel:** Disclosure recommended; recusal only if hostility or ongoing ties exist.
5. **Social media connections:** Passive connections

require disclosure; active engagement may require recusal.

Cross-References

See Chapter 4 (Family Members and Conflicts of Interest) for related analysis of close personal ties, and Chapter 14 (Social Media: Campaign Use) for further treatment of online relationships.

Authorities & String Cites

- **Social acquaintances** — *Fla. JEAC Op.* 1995-21 (July 14, 1995); *Fla. JEAC Op.* 2008-12 (June 12, 2008).
- **Close personal friends** — *Fla. JEAC Op.* 1998-23 (Aug. 28, 1998); *Fla. JEAC Op.* 2010-25 (Dec. 20, 2010).
- **Former law partners** — *Fla. JEAC Op.* 2002-15 (June 6, 2002); *Fla. JEAC Op.* 2016-08 (July 14, 2016).
- **Former opposing counsel** — *Fla. JEAC Op.* 1999-15 (Aug. 13, 1999); *Fla. JEAC Op.* 2007-14 (Sept. 7, 2007).
- **Social media friendships** — *Fla. JEAC*

Op. 2009-20 (Oct. 9, 2009); *Fla. JEAC Op.* 2012-12 (May 31, 2012).

Canon Anchors (for quick lookup)

Canon 2; Canon 3E(1); Canon 3E(1)(a)–(d); Canon 5C(1).

Chapter 7

Ex Parte Communications

Introduction

Few ethical issues carry as much immediate weight as ex parte communications. An ex parte communication is any contact between judge and one side of a matter, without the other side's knowledge or opportunity to participate. Even a seemingly harmless exchange — a letter, an email, a hallway comment — can undermine public confidence in neutrality. The Canons recognize narrow exceptions for scheduling, administrative matters, and emergency situations, but the general rule is strict:

judges must not initiate, permit, or consider ex parte communications about substantive issues in pending or impending matters. The JEAC has repeatedly emphasized that judges must not only avoid ex parte communications but must also instruct staff and court officials under their direction to do the same. Judges who receive such communications must disclose them promptly, place them on the record, and provide opposing parties a fair opportunity to respond. This chapter collects scenarios where ex parte communications arise most often: informal letters from parties, attorneys seeking private clarification, communications through staff, and emergency contacts.

Core Canon anchors. Canon 3B(7) establishes the central rule: a judge must not initiate, permit, or consider ex parte communications concerning pending or impending matters, subject only to specific exceptions for scheduling, administrative matters, settlement conferences with consent, and authorized communications by law. Canon 2A and 2B provide the broader principle that impartiality must not only exist but be seen to exist; undisclosed communications erode trust even if they do not affect the outcome. Canon 3C(2) requires judges to demand the same standard of conduct from staff, judicial assistants, and bailiffs, extending the ex parte prohibition to those who serve under the judge's direction. Canon 3B(8) adds that judges must promptly disclose on the record any ex parte communication received, giving the parties an opportunity to respond. Together these Canons form a bright-line system: avoid private communications about substantive matters, allow limited administrative communications with disclosure, and always place anything received into the record.

Scenario A: Letter from a pro se litigant

A self-represented party sends you a letter detailing their side of a case, asking for special consideration.

What the JEAC Said (summary)

Judges must not read or act upon such letters. The letter should be filed in the case docket, disclosed to all parties, and treated as an improper ex parte communication. No ruling should be based on the content unless both sides have had an opportunity to respond.

Key Takeaway

Do not privately consider letters or communications from parties; place them in the record and notify all parties.

Authorities

Fla. JEAC Op. 1997-13 (July 18, 1997); *Fla. JEAC Op.* 2005-07 (May 5, 2005).

Scenario B: Attorney's "quick question" in chambers

An attorney appearing before you stops by chambers to ask about a ruling in their pending case.

What the JEAC Said (summary)

Any discussion of substantive issues outside the presence of opposing counsel is prohibited. Even if the question seems procedural, the safe course is to decline discussion and instruct the attorney to file a motion or request on the record. Casual "clarifications" in chambers create the appearance of back-channel influence.

Key Takeaway

Never entertain substantive questions from counsel outside the presence of opposing parties; redirect all requests to the record.

Authorities

Fla. JEAC Op. 1999-16 (Aug. 20, 1999); *Fla. JEAC Op.* 2011-05 (Apr. 21, 2011).

Scenario C: Communications through staff

Your judicial assistant receives a phone call from a lawyer seeking guidance on how you might view a pending evidentiary motion.

What the JEAC Said (summary)

Staff are bound by the same restrictions as judges. Judicial assistants must not convey, solicit, or receive ex parte information about cases. Judges have an affirmative duty to train and instruct staff accordingly.

Key Takeaway

Judicial staff cannot act as intermediaries for ex parte contacts; judges must set and enforce strict chambers policies.

Authorities

Fla. JEAC Op. 2000-08 (July 27, 2000); *Fla. JEAC Op.* 2014-05 (Mar. 20, 2014).

Scenario D: Emergency contact

Late at night, law enforcement contacts you directly by phone, seeking emergency approval of a search warrant.

What the JEAC Said (summary)

Ex parte communications specifically authorized by law, such as review of search warrant applications, are permissible. The judge must limit discussion to the statutory framework, avoid unrelated topics, and ensure the record is created as required.

Key Takeaway

Ex parte communications are permitted when expressly authorized by law (e.g., warrants), but

must be narrow, recorded, and limited to legal requirements.

Authorities

Fla. JEAC Op. 2003-10 (May 30, 2003); *Fla. JEAC Op.* 2018-11 (July 12, 2018).

Scenario E: Settlement conferences

Parties request that you meet privately with each side, at different times, to encourage settlement.

What the JEAC Said (summary)

Judges may conduct settlement conferences only with the informed consent of the parties, and communications must remain focused on settlement, not the merits of unresolved issues. Without consent, such conferences risk violating the ex parte rule.

Key Takeaway

Settlement discussions require party consent and must remain confined to settlement issues; absent consent, avoid private caucuses.

Authorities

Fla. JEAC Op. 1996-10 (May 24, 1996); *Fla. JEAC Op.* 2010-11 (June 17, 2010).

Practical Checklist: Ex Parte Communications

1. **Is it substantive?** If yes, prohibit and redirect to the record.
2. **Is it administrative?** Limited communications are permissible for scheduling or emergencies, with disclosure to all parties.
3. **Is it staff-related?** Train staff to apply the same prohibition; no back-channel communications allowed.
4. **Is it legally authorized?** If the law permits (e.g., warrants), keep it narrow and make a record.
5. **Always disclose:** Place any ex parte communication on the record and notify the other parties promptly.

Cross-References

See Chapter 6 (Disqualification: Friendships and Former Colleagues) for overlap on impartiality, and Chapter 8 (Courtroom Demeanor and Commentary) for related concerns about informal exchanges.

Authorities & String Cites

- **Letters from litigants** — *Fla. JEAC Op.* 1997-13 (July 18, 1997); *Fla. JEAC Op.* 2005-07 (May 5, 2005).
- **Attorney "quick questions"** — *Fla. JEAC Op.* 1999-16 (Aug. 20, 1999); *Fla. JEAC Op.* 2011-05 (Apr. 21, 2011).
- **Staff as intermediaries** — *Fla. JEAC Op.* 2000-08 (July 27, 2000); *Fla. JEAC Op.* 2014-05 (Mar. 20, 2014).
- **Emergency contacts** — *Fla. JEAC Op.* 2003-10 (May 30, 2003); *Fla. JEAC Op.* 2018-11 (July 12, 2018).
- **Settlement conferences** — *Fla. JEAC Op.* 1996-10 (May 24, 1996); *Fla. JEAC Op.* 2010-11 (June 17, 2010).

Canon Anchors (for quick lookup)

Canon 2; Canon 3B(7); Canon 3B(8); Canon 3C(2).

Chapter 8

Courtroom Demeanor and Commentary

Introduction

The authority of the judiciary rests not only on rulings but also on how judges carry themselves in the courtroom. Demeanor — tone, word choice, gestures, and commentary — can affirm fairness or, if misused, erode it. Litigants, attorneys, jurors, and the public watch carefully; a stray remark or cutting comment can fuel perceptions of bias, ridicule, or hostility. The Canons recognize that judges are human, but they impose heightened restraint. Judges must be patient, dignified, and courteous, even in the face of provocation. The JEAC has cautioned that humor, sarcasm, or commentary on the merits of cases, whether inside or outside the courtroom, can create lasting doubts about impartiality. This chapter reviews scenarios where courtroom demeanor and commentary most often cross ethical lines: remarks about parties or counsel, public comments about pending cases, judicial humor, and interactions with jurors. The theme is consistent: dignity and restraint are not optional; they are the essence of judicial office.

Core Canon anchors. Canon 3B(4) requires judges to be patient, dignified, and courteous to litigants, jurors, witnesses, lawyers, and others with whom the judge deals. Canon 2A instructs judges to act at all times in a manner that promotes public confidence in impartiality, which includes refraining from sarcastic, belittling, or demeaning comments. Canon 3B(5) prohibits manifestations of bias or prejudice, whether based on race, gender, socioeconomic status, or other protected characteristics. Canon 3B(9) bars judges from commenting publicly on pending or impending matters, whether from the bench, in the press, or in public speeches. Canon 3C(2) obligates judges to require staff and officials under their direction to observe the same standards, extending courtesy and restraint throughout the court. Together these provisions create a framework that goes beyond silence: they require affirmative dignity. Judges must show restraint not only when delivering rulings but in every interaction that reflects on the integrity of the judicial system.

Scenario A: Sarcastic comments to counsel

During oral argument, you make a sarcastic remark mocking an attorney's presentation.

What the JEAC Said (summary)

The Committee has consistently advised that sarcasm, ridicule, or humor at the expense of counsel undermines public confidence in impartiality. Even if the comment is meant lightly, it can appear demeaning and create a record for appeal. Judges are expected to maintain dignity and courtesy at all times.

Key Takeaway

Avoid sarcasm or ridicule in the courtroom; courtesy is not optional but required.

Authorities

Fla. JEAC Op. 1997-18 (Sept. 5, 1997); *Fla. JEAC Op.* 2008-07 (Apr. 24, 2008).

Scenario B: Judicial humor

You inject humor into a hearing, joking about a litigant's claim.

What the JEAC Said (summary)

Judicial humor is not forbidden, but it must never be at a party's expense. Comments that seem to belittle, mock, or dismiss a claim create an appearance of bias. Humor must be directed inward or toward light procedural moments, not substantive rights.

Key Takeaway

Humor in the courtroom must be carefully limited; never joke about litigants, counsel, or the merits of a case.

Authorities

Fla. JEAC Op. 2003-12 (June 27, 2003); *Fla. JEAC Op.* 2011-09 (May 19, 2011).

Scenario C: Public comments on pending cases

At a bar association luncheon, you comment on the strength of evidence in a high-profile case pending before another division.

What the JEAC Said (summary)

Canon 3B(9) strictly prohibits public commentary on pending or impending cases, whether in one's own courtroom or another's. Even general observations can be perceived as prejudging. Judges may discuss procedure or legal education in general terms but must avoid case-specific remarks.

Key Takeaway

Never publicly comment on pending cases; restrict remarks to general legal education and avoid substantive commentary.

Authorities

Fla. JEAC Op. 1999-12 (June 11, 1999); *Fla. JEAC Op.* 2015-07 (Apr. 16, 2015).

Scenario D: Interaction with jurors

Following a trial, you chat with jurors in chambers, thanking them but also commenting on the strength of the evidence.

What the JEAC Said (summary)

While thanking jurors for their service is permissible, commentary on the evidence or verdict is improper. Such remarks can undermine the perception of neutrality and may discourage honest deliberations in future cases. Interactions with jurors must remain dignified, respectful, and free from substantive case discussion.

Key Takeaway

Thank jurors for service but avoid commenting on evidence, deliberations, or verdicts.

Authorities

Fla. JEAC Op. 2000-19 (Aug. 11, 2000); *Fla. JEAC Op.* 2012-06 (Apr. 19, 2012).

Scenario E: Commentary on litigants' credibility

From the bench, you remark that one litigant "obviously lied" during testimony.

What the JEAC Said (summary)

While judges must make credibility determinations, announcing them in a demeaning way undermines dignity. Findings should be made in rulings or orders, not through disparaging commentary during proceedings. The Committee advises against language that humiliates or ridicules litigants.

Key Takeaway

Credibility findings belong in rulings, not disparaging bench commentary; avoid humiliating parties in open court.

Authorities

Fla. JEAC Op. 1996-09 (Apr. 26, 1996); *Fla. JEAC Op.* 2009-11 (July 2, 2009).

Practical Checklist: Demeanor and Commentary

1. **Maintain dignity:** Courtesy, patience, and respect are required in every interaction.
2. **Avoid ridicule:** Sarcasm, mockery, or belittling comments undermine impartiality.
3. **Use humor cautiously:** Safe only when neutral and non-demeaning.
4. **No public commentary:** Never discuss pending or impending cases outside the courtroom.
5. **Respect jurors:** Express gratitude without discussing evidence or deliberations.
6. **Focus credibility findings:** State them in written rulings, not off-hand remarks.

Cross-References

See Chapter 7 (Ex Parte Communications) for overlap on improper remarks outside proceedings, and Chapter 13 (Social Media: Personal Accounts) for commentary issues in online contexts.

Authorities & String Cites

- **Sarcastic comments** — *Fla. JEAC Op*. 1997-18 (Sept. 5, 1997); *Fla. JEAC Op*. 2008-07 (Apr. 24, 2008).
- **Judicial humor** — *Fla. JEAC Op*. 2003-12 (June 27, 2003); *Fla. JEAC Op*. 2011-09 (May 19, 2011).
- **Public case comments** — *Fla. JEAC Op*. 1999-12 (June 11, 1999); *Fla. JEAC Op*. 2015-07 (Apr. 16, 2015).
- **Interaction with jurors** — *Fla. JEAC Op*. 2000-19 (Aug. 11, 2000); *Fla. JEAC Op*. 2012-06 (Apr. 19, 2012).
- **Litigant credibility remarks** — *Fla. JEAC Op*. 1996-09 (Apr. 26, 1996); *Fla. JEAC Op*. 2009-11 (July 2, 2009).

Canon Anchors (for quick lookup)

Canon 2; Canon 3B(4); Canon 3B(5); Canon 3B(9); Canon 3C(2).

Chapter 9

Campaign Speech and Endorsements

Introduction

Judicial campaigns occupy a unique space in the democratic process. Unlike other candidates, judicial candidates must engage voters without becoming partisan advocates. They must raise funds, communicate qualifications, and speak to civic groups — all while maintaining the independence, integrity, and impartiality of the judiciary. The Florida JEAC has repeatedly cautioned that campaign speech cannot drift into promises about future rulings, partisan advocacy, or endorsements of other candidates. At the same time, candidates are encouraged to share their background, judicial philosophy, and commitment to the rule of law. The recurring challenges include: how to participate in civic forums, whether to respond to questionnaires, how to handle requests for endorsements, whether ideological labels are permissible, and how to avoid impermissible political donations. This chapter surveys those issues through scenarios and the JEAC's interpretive guidance.

Core Canon anchors. Canon 7A(3)(d)(i) prohibits judicial candidates from making statements that commit or appear to commit them on issues likely to come before the court. Canon 7A(3)(d)(ii) bars misrepresentations of facts, qualifications, or present positions during campaigns. Canon 7C(3) prohibits judges and judicial candidates from publicly endorsing or opposing other candidates for office, except in very narrow family-related circumstances. Canon 7A(1)(d) further prohibits judges from engaging in political activity inappropriate to judicial office, which includes making contributions to partisan politicians or parties. Canon 7C(2) restricts campaign activity to one's own race, forbidding contributions to other judicial candidates. Canon 2 serves as the ever-present safeguard, requiring judges to avoid both actual impropriety and the appearance of impropriety. Taken together, these provisions draw a narrow path: judicial candidates may educate voters about their qualifications and philosophy, but must never commit to outcomes, align with political parties, or engage in fundraising for anyone but themselves.

Scenario A: Speaking at civic forums

You are invited to speak at a local civic club about your candidacy. The organizers want to know your "position" on specific public policy issues.

What the JEAC Said (summary)

Candidates may attend civic forums and discuss qualifications, experience, and the role of the judiciary. They may not express commitments on issues likely to come before the court. The line between educating and promising is critical: once speech suggests predisposition, it crosses into prohibited territory.

Key Takeaway

Discuss qualifications and judicial philosophy; do not state positions on issues likely to arise in court.

Authorities

Fla. JEAC Op. 2000-23 (Sept. 14, 2000); *Fla. JEAC Op.* 2014-04 (Mar. 6, 2014).

Scenario B: Endorsing another candidate

A long-time friend is running for city commission and asks you to publicly endorse her campaign.

What the JEAC Said (summary)

Judges and judicial candidates may not endorse other candidates for public office. This rule applies regardless of friendship or personal loyalty. The integrity of the judiciary requires separation from partisan contests.

Key Takeaway

Judges may not endorse or oppose candidates for other offices, even when close friends or colleagues are involved.

Authorities

Fla. JEAC Op. 1998-12 (May 7, 1998); *Fla. JEAC Op.* 2011-13 (June 23, 2011).

Scenario C: Responding to questionnaires

You receive a questionnaire from a local political group asking for your views on criminal justice reform.

What the JEAC Said (summary)

Candidates may not answer questionnaires that seek commitments on issues likely to come before the court. Even indirect answers suggesting a predisposition create ethical concerns. Candidates may respond by explaining why the Canons prohibit them from answering.

Key Takeaway

Do not respond to questionnaires on substantive issues; explain that the Canons prohibit such commitments.

Authorities

Fla. JEAC Op. 1996-21 (Aug. 30, 1996); *Fla. JEAC Op.* 2007-17 (Oct. 4, 2007).

Scenario D: Speaking about personal background

At a candidate forum, you are asked about your upbringing, career path, and family values.

What the JEAC Said (summary)

Candidates may share biographical information and personal history so long as it is truthful and does not misrepresent qualifications. The Committee has encouraged candidates to emphasize experience, character, and judicial philosophy rather than political views.

Key Takeaway

Biographical and experiential statements are permitted; ensure all representations are accurate and avoid political framing.

Authorities

Fla. JEAC Op. 1995-10 (Apr. 7, 1995); *Fla. JEAC Op.* 2009-12 (July 9, 2009).

Scenario E: Endorsements from organizations

A local law enforcement union wishes to endorse your candidacy publicly.

What the JEAC Said (summary)

Judicial candidates may not seek or accept endorsements from partisan political organizations or groups that regularly appear in court. Accepting such endorsements creates the impression of indebtedness and undermines neutrality.

Key Takeaway

Do not seek or accept endorsements from partisan or advocacy organizations; independence must remain clear.

Authorities

Fla. JEAC Op. 2002-07 (Mar. 15, 2002); *Fla. JEAC Op.* 2016-05 (May 26, 2016)

Scenario F: Judge donating to another judicial candidate

You are asked to contribute financially to the campaign of a colleague who is seeking reelection to the bench.

What the JEAC Said (summary)

Judges and judicial candidates may not make financial contributions to other judicial candidates. Canon 7C(2) restricts political activity by judges to their own campaigns, and contributions to fellow judges create the appearance of political alliances within the judiciary. Even modest donations risk signaling partiality or indebtedness.

Key Takeaway

Judges may not donate to the campaigns of other judicial candidates; campaign activity is limited strictly to one's own race.

Authorities

Fla. JEAC Op. 2004-19 (Sept. 23, 2004); *Fla. JEAC Op.* 2010-09 (May 6, 2010).

Scenario G: Judge donating to partisan politicians

A sitting judge wishes to contribute to the gubernatorial campaign of a longtime family friend, or to a political party's fundraising event.

What the JEAC Said (summary)

Judges may not contribute to partisan political candidates or parties. Canon 7A(1)(d) prohibits judges from engaging in political activity inappropriate to judicial office, and contributions are considered political activity. Allowing judges to donate would undermine the strict neutrality required of the judiciary.

Key Takeaway

Judges are prohibited from donating to partisan politicians or political parties; doing so constitutes impermissible political activity.

Authorities

Fla. JEAC Op. 1997-21 (Sept. 19, 1997); *Fla. JEAC Op.* 2015-05 (Apr. 2, 2015).

Scenario H: Campaign materials using ideological language

During your campaign, you distributed brochures describing yourself as "conservative" and highlighting positions that many voters might associate with Republican platforms. A complaint is filed alleging impermissible partisan activity.

What the JEAC Said (summary)

The Committee has drawn a distinction between impermissible partisan activity and broad philosophical descriptors. Judges may not campaign as the candidate of a political party or align themselves with partisan agendas. However, describing one's judicial philosophy in general terms — such as "conservative," "strict constructionist," or "committed to traditional values" — is not automatically a violation if the statements are framed in a way that emphasizes judicial method and impartiality rather than partisan identity. The key question is whether a reasonable observer would view the materials as an alignment with a political party, or instead as a description of judicial philosophy.

Key Takeaway

Judicial candidates may describe their philosophy in general terms, but must avoid partisan labels or language that ties them directly to a political party. The distinction rests on whether the messaging aligns with a method of judging or with party platforms.

Authorities

Fla. JEAC Op. 2002-18 (Sept. 13, 2002); *Fla. JEAC Op.* 2013-07 (May 2, 2013).

Practical Checklist: Campaign Speech and Endorsements

1. **Stay within qualifications:** Speak about background, experience, character, and judicial philosophy — not positions on disputed legal or political issues.

2. **Use of ideology:** Broad descriptors such as "conservative," "strict constructionist," or

"committed to fairness" may be permissible if framed as judicial philosophy, not partisan identity. Avoid language that ties the campaign to a political party or platform.

3. **Avoid endorsements:** Do not endorse or oppose other candidates for any office, including judicial colleagues.
4. **No promises:** Never commit to outcomes or positions on issues likely to come before the court.
5. **Respond carefully:** Decline questionnaires seeking issue commitments; explain that ethical rules prevent such answers.
6. **Donations:** Do not donate to other judicial candidates or partisan politicians; campaign activity is limited to one's own race.
7. **Accept only neutral platforms:** Appear at civic or community events only when they are nonpartisan, broadly open, and unrelated to partisan advocacy.

Commentary

Campaign speech is a narrow corridor. Judicial candidates must provide voters with enough information to make informed choices, yet remain firmly outside the world of partisan politics. The JEAC has recognized that judges may describe their approach to judging in broad, philosophical terms, but may not present themselves as aligned with political parties or platforms. The safest course is to frame all campaign messaging around judicial philosophy, experience, integrity, and the impartial role of the judiciary. By walking this careful line, judges preserve the confidence of voters without compromising the independence of the courts.

Authorities & String Cites

- **Civic forums and issues** — *Fla. JEAC Op.* 2000-23 (Sept. 14, 2000); *Fla. JEAC Op.* 2014-04 (Mar. 6, 2014).
- **Endorsing another candidate** — *Fla. JEAC Op.* 1998-12 (May 7, 1998); *Fla. JEAC Op.* 2011-13 (June 23, 2011).
- **Questionnaires** — *Fla. JEAC Op.* 1996-21 (Aug. 30, 1996); *Fla. JEAC Op.* 2007-17 (Oct. 4, 2007).
- **Personal background** — *Fla. JEAC Op.* 1995-10 (Apr. 7, 1995); *Fla. JEAC Op.* 2009-12 (July 9, 2009).
- **Organizational endorsements** — *Fla. JEAC*

Op. 2002-07 (Mar. 15, 2002); *Fla. JEAC Op.* 2016-05 (May 26, 2016).

- **Donations to judicial candidates** — *Fla. JEAC Op.* 2004-19 (Sept. 23, 2004); *Fla. JEAC Op.* 2010-09 (May 6, 2010).
- **Donations to partisan politicians** — *Fla. JEAC Op.* 1997-21 (Sept. 19, 1997); *Fla. JEAC Op.* 2015-05 (Apr. 2, 2015).
- **Use of ideological terms in campaign materials** — *Fla. JEAC Op.* 2002-18 (Sept. 13, 2002); *Fla. JEAC Op.* 2013-07 (May 2, 2013).

Canon Anchors (for quick lookup)

Canon 2; Canon 7A(1)(d); Canon 7A(3)(d)(i)–(ii); Canon 7C(2); Canon 7C(3).

Chapter 10

Campaign Finance Rules

Introduction

Fundraising is an unavoidable reality of judicial elections, but it is also one of the most tightly regulated aspects of judicial conduct. The Canons strike a balance: judicial candidates must raise money to run campaigns, yet they must avoid any perception that financial support buys access or influence. Unlike other candidates, judges may not personally solicit or accept contributions. Campaign committees may do so on the judge's behalf within strict limits, and all contributions must be transparent and reported. The JEAC has addressed recurring questions: who may solicit funds, how committees must operate, whether judges may attend fundraising events, what to do with surplus funds, and how to treat loans or self-funding. The guiding principle remains constant: judicial fundraising must be conducted in a way that safeguards impartiality and maintains public confidence in the independence of the judiciary.

Core Canon anchors. Canon 7C(1) prohibits judges and judicial candidates from personally soliciting campaign funds or accepting contributions. Instead, candidates must establish campaign committees to handle fundraising activity. Canon 7C(2) prohibits judges from making political contributions to other judges or candidates, reinforcing that campaign finance activity is strictly limited to one's own race. Canon 7A(1)(d) bars judges from engaging in partisan political fundraising, including attending partisan events or contributing to political parties. Canon 7C(3) restricts endorsements and associations with partisan fundraising efforts, requiring judges to remain neutral and above the appearance of political indebtedness. Canon 2 serves as the overarching principle: even lawful contributions must be managed to avoid the appearance that litigants or lawyers can buy favor through donations. Read together, these Canons create a strict framework: campaign fundraising must be handled exclusively by committees, conducted in compliance with state law, and always transparent to avoid undermining judicial impartiality.

Scenario A: Personal solicitation

You consider writing personal letters to colleagues and attorneys you know, asking them to contribute to your campaign.

What the JEAC Said (summary)

Judges and judicial candidates are absolutely prohibited from personally soliciting funds. This includes direct letters, emails, or phone calls. All solicitation must be conducted through an authorized campaign committee.

Key Takeaway

Judges may not personally solicit campaign funds; all fundraising must go through a committee.

Authorities

Fla. JEAC Op. 1995-15 (May 26, 1995); *Fla. JEAC Op.* 2006-09 (June 2, 2006).

Scenario B: Fundraising dinners and events

A local civic group offers to host a dinner in your honor, with ticket sales to support your campaign.

What the JEAC Said (summary)

Fundraising events may be held on behalf of judicial candidates, but the candidate must not personally solicit contributions or sell tickets. The campaign committee may organize and promote the event, but the judge's appearance must be carefully limited to avoid direct solicitation.

Key Takeaway

Judicial candidates may attend campaign events, but all solicitation and ticket sales must be handled exclusively by the campaign committee.

Authorities

Fla. JEAC Op. 2001-08 (Apr. 20, 2001); *Fla. JEAC Op.* 2012-15 (Sept. 6, 2012).

Scenario C: Loans and self-funding

You plan to loan your campaign $50,000 from personal funds.

What the JEAC Said (summary)

Self-funding through loans or direct contributions is permissible under both the Canons and Florida election law. Such funding must be reported, and repayments must be handled transparently. The restriction is on soliciting others, not on contributing one's own resources.

Key Takeaway

Judges may self-fund their campaigns by loan or contribution, but must disclose and report all amounts as required by law.

Authorities

Fla. JEAC Op. 1997-17 (Aug. 8, 1997); *Fla. JEAC Op.* 2015-09 (June 4, 2015).

Scenario D: Surplus campaign funds

At the conclusion of your campaign, you have surplus funds left in the campaign account.

What the JEAC Said (summary)

Surplus funds must be disposed of according to Florida election law, such as donation to the state, contribution to a political party only if permitted by statute (not encouraged under the Canons), refund to contributors, or transfer to a trust fund for future campaigns as allowed. The Canons require strict compliance with statutory procedures to prevent misuse.

Key Takeaway

Handle surplus funds exactly as permitted by statute; improper distribution risks both legal and ethical violations.

Authorities

Fla. JEAC Op. 2000-12 (June 15, 2000); *Fla. JEAC Op.* 2018-09 (May 24, 2018).

Scenario E: Attending partisan fundraising events

You are invited to attend a partisan political party's annual fundraising banquet as a guest.

What the JEAC Said (summary)

Judges may not attend partisan fundraising events. Attendance is considered political activity inconsistent with judicial neutrality, even if the judge does not speak or contribute.

Key Takeaway

Judges may not attend partisan political fundraising events under any circumstance.

Authorities

Fla. JEAC Op. 1996-18 (July 19, 1996); *Fla. JEAC Op.* 2013-11 (July 18, 2013).

Scenario F: Contributions from attorneys appearing before you

A lawyer who frequently practices in your division makes a substantial contribution to your campaign.

What the JEAC Said (summary)

Such contributions are permissible under Florida law, but they create strong appearance concerns. Disclosure is always required, and recusal may be necessary depending on timing, size, and circumstances, as discussed in Chapter 5.

Key Takeaway

Contributions from attorneys are legally permissible but raise serious appearance concerns; disclosure is mandatory and recusal may be required.

Authorities

Fla. JEAC Op. 2000-27 (Oct. 26, 2000); *Fla. JEAC Op.* 2016-13 (Aug. 18, 2016).

Practical Checklist: Fundraising and Campaign Finance

1. **No personal solicitation:** All fundraising must go through an authorized campaign committee.
2. **Campaign events:** Judges may attend, but must not sell tickets or request contributions.
3. **Self-funding:** Permitted, but must be reported as required by law.
4. **Surplus funds:** Dispose of them strictly according to statute.
5. **Partisan events:** Never attend or participate in partisan political fundraising.
6. **Attorney contributions:** Acceptable by law, but always disclose and consider recusal depending on timing and size.

Commentary

Fundraising rules exist to protect the core of judicial independence. Unlike other candidates, judges cannot personally ask for money because the act of solicitation itself could imply coercion to lawyers and litigants who appear in court. Campaign committees serve as a buffer, creating separation between donors and judges. Even then, transparency and restraint are essential. The public must never believe that justice can be purchased. By adhering closely to the Canons, judges ensure that campaign fundraising sustains — rather than erodes — public confidence in the judiciary.

Authorities & String Cites

- **Personal solicitation** — *Fla. JEAC Op.* 1995-15 (May 26, 1995); *Fla. JEAC Op.* 2006-09 (June 2, 2006).
- **Fundraising events** — *Fla. JEAC Op.* 2001-08 (Apr. 20, 2001); *Fla. JEAC Op.* 2012-15 (Sept. 6, 2012).
- **Self-funding / loans** — *Fla. JEAC Op.* 1997-17 (Aug. 8, 1997); *Fla. JEAC Op.* 2015-09 (June 4, 2015).
- **Surplus funds** — *Fla. JEAC Op.* 2000-12 (June 15, 2000); *Fla. JEAC Op.* 2018-09 (May 24, 2018).
- **Partisan events** — *Fla. JEAC Op.* 1996-18 (July 19, 1996); *Fla. JEAC Op.* 2013-11 (July 18, 2013).
- **Attorney contributions** — *Fla. JEAC Op.* 2000-27 (Oct. 26, 2000); *Fla. JEAC*

Op. 2016-13 (Aug. 18, 2016).

Canon Anchors (for quick lookup)

Canon 2; Canon 7A(1)(d); Canon 7C(1)–(3).

Chapter 11

Civic and Religious Activities

Introduction

Judges are encouraged to participate in civic life, but their role carries limits that ensure impartiality and protect the prestige of judicial office from being used for private gain. Service on nonprofit boards, charitable organizations, or religious institutions can strengthen community ties and model public engagement. At the same time, these activities can expose judges to conflicts of interest, fundraising concerns, or perceived political alliances. The Canons permit judges to engage in civic, charitable, and religious activities, provided such involvement does not reflect adversely on judicial impartiality or interfere with judicial duties. Judges must also avoid becoming involved in organizations that are likely to appear in court or that engage in political advocacy. This chapter explores scenarios involving board membership, fundraising, participation in religious activities, and public advocacy through nonprofit affiliations.

Core Canon anchors. Canon 5C(3) authorizes judges to participate in civic and charitable activities not conducted for profit, but restricts involvement where the organization is likely to be engaged in proceedings before the court or regularly involved in adversarial matters. Canon 5C(3)(b)(i) prohibits judges from personally soliciting funds for charitable organizations, even those they serve as officers or directors, though they may be listed on letterhead if other members are listed. Canon 5C(3)(b)(ii) prohibits judges from using the prestige of judicial office to advance the interests of others. Canon 5C(3)(b)(iii) allows judges to assist in planning fundraising and management but bars personal participation in solicitation. Canon 2A and 2B provide the broader framework, reminding judges that even permissible service must not create the appearance of partiality, favoritism, or endorsement of particular causes. Together, these Canons permit judges to contribute to their communities while drawing firm boundaries around fundraising, political advocacy, and associations that may erode public confidence in impartiality.

Scenario A: Serving on a nonprofit board

You are invited to serve on the board of a local domestic violence shelter that occasionally partners with law enforcement and appears in grant-related hearings.

What the JEAC Said (summary)

Judges may serve on boards of charitable organizations that are not frequently engaged in adversarial proceedings before the court. However, if the shelter regularly appears in cases, the judge's service would create conflicts. Judges must carefully evaluate the frequency of the organization's court involvement before accepting such roles.

Key Takeaway

Judges may serve on nonprofit boards only if the organization is not likely to appear regularly in

court; otherwise conflicts of interest arise.

Authorities

Fla. JEAC Op. 1998-19 (July 24, 1998); *Fla. JEAC Op.* 2011-16 (July 21, 2011).

Scenario B: Charitable fundraising

You are asked to be the keynote speaker at a fundraising gala for a local legal aid society.

What the JEAC Said (summary)

Judges may attend charitable events but may not be featured speakers if the event's purpose is fundraising. Judicial participation may lend prestige to the event and constitute impermissible solicitation. Judges may support the organization privately or in non-fundraising contexts.

Key Takeaway

Judges may not serve as speakers or featured guests at fundraising events; presence is allowed only if it does not imply solicitation.

Authorities

Fla. JEAC Op. 2000-05 (Mar. 9, 2000); *Fla. JEAC Op.* 2013-06 (May 9, 2013).

Scenario C: Religious leadership

You are asked to serve as an elder in your local church, which sometimes advocates publicly on social policy issues.

What the JEAC Said (summary)

Judges may participate in religious activities and hold leadership positions, provided the role does not involve fundraising or political advocacy. If the religious organization takes public stances on controversial legal or political matters, the judge must decline visible leadership roles that could tie the judiciary to advocacy.

Key Takeaway

Judges may hold religious leadership roles if limited to spiritual functions and free from fundraising or political advocacy.

Authorities

Fla. JEAC Op. 1999-20 (Oct. 22, 1999); *Fla. JEAC Op.* 2015-11 (July 23, 2015).

Scenario D: Civic club membership

You are invited to join a civic club that occasionally endorses political candidates and issues.

What the JEAC Said (summary)

Judges may not join organizations that engage in political endorsements or advocacy. Membership would link the judge to partisan positions inconsistent with judicial neutrality. Social and civic clubs with no political activity remain permissible.

Key Takeaway

Judges may not join civic organizations that endorse political candidates or advocate for partisan causes.

Authorities

Fla. JEAC Op. 2002-13 (May 24, 2002); *Fla. JEAC Op.* 2017-12 (Sept. 21, 2017).

Scenario E: Advisory role in nonprofit fundraising

You are asked to serve on a nonprofit's advisory committee, helping design fundraising strategy but not directly soliciting funds.

What the JEAC Said (summary)

Judges may assist in planning fundraising as long as they do not personally solicit funds or allow their judicial office to be used for solicitation. Care must be taken that advisory involvement is not perceived as judicial endorsement.

Key Takeaway

Judges may help plan fundraising but must not solicit or lend the prestige of judicial office to campaigns.

Authorities

Fla. JEAC Op. 1997-15 (Aug. 15, 1997); *Fla. JEAC Op.* 2008-09 (May 8, 2008).

Practical Checklist: Civic, Charitable, and Religious Activities

1. **Board service:** Accept only if the organization is unlikely to appear in court.
2. **Fundraising:** Never personally solicit or serve as featured speaker at fundraising events.
3. **Religious leadership:** Permissible if limited to spiritual roles and not tied to advocacy or fundraising.
4. **Civic memberships:** Avoid organizations engaged in political endorsements or advocacy.
5. **Advisory roles:** Planning is allowed, but solicitation and visible judicial endorsement are prohibited.

Commentary

Civic and charitable engagement helps judges remain connected to their communities, but it must be carefully bounded. The risk lies not only in actual conflicts of interest but in the perception that judicial prestige is being leveraged for fundraising or political causes. The

Canons allow judges to contribute time and talent, provided they avoid solicitation, partisan involvement, and organizations that appear before the courts. The safest path is transparency and restraint, ensuring that civic service complements rather than compromises judicial independence.

Authorities & String Cites

- **Nonprofit board service** — *Fla. JEAC Op.* 1998-19 (July 24, 1998); *Fla. JEAC Op.* 2011-16 (July 21, 2011).
- **Charitable fundraising** — *Fla. JEAC Op.* 2000-05 (Mar. 9, 2000); *Fla. JEAC Op.* 2013-06 (May 9, 2013).
- **Religious leadership** — *Fla. JEAC Op.* 1999-20 (Oct. 22, 1999); *Fla. JEAC Op.* 2015-11 (July 23, 2015).
- **Civic club membership** — *Fla. JEAC Op.* 2002-13 (May 24, 2002); *Fla. JEAC Op.* 2017-12 (Sept. 21, 2017).
- **Advisory fundraising roles** — *Fla. JEAC Op.* 1997-15 (Aug. 15, 1997); *Fla. JEAC Op.* 2008-09 (May 8, 2008).

Canon Anchors (for quick lookup)

Canon 2; Canon 5C(3); Canon 5C(3)(b)(i)–(iii).

Chapter 12

Bar Association Activities

Introduction

Participation in bar associations and professional organizations is an important aspect of judicial service. These organizations provide a forum for legal education, law reform, and collegial exchange. Judges are encouraged to contribute to these efforts, but must remain vigilant to avoid activities that compromise impartiality, resemble advocacy, or blur the separation between bench and bar. The JEAC has advised on recurring issues: serving in leadership roles, speaking at bar events, participating in continuing legal education (CLE), joining specialty or affinity bar associations, and contributing to professional publications. The constant thread is balance — judges may support the profession but must not lend judicial prestige to advance private interests or align with groups engaged in advocacy that may appear in court.

Core Canon anchors. Canon 4A encourages judges to engage in activities that improve the law, the legal system, and the administration of justice. Canon 4B authorizes judges to speak, write, lecture, and participate in educational programs concerning the law, provided such activities do not interfere with judicial duties or cast doubt on impartiality. Canon 5C(3) permits service in legal and professional organizations, but limits such participation if the organization is engaged in proceedings that would ordinarily come before the court. Canon 2 warns judges not to lend the prestige of their office to advance the interests of others, including bar groups with advocacy agendas. Together, these Canons set a framework: judges may serve, speak, and write in professional circles, but must remain cautious about advocacy, fundraising, and partisanship.

Scenario A: Leadership in a voluntary bar association

You are asked to serve as president of your county bar association.

What the JEAC Said (summary)

Judges may hold leadership positions in voluntary bar associations. However, judges must avoid involvement in the association's political or lobbying efforts, particularly if the group takes positions on contested legal issues. Participation should focus on educational, professional development, and administrative functions.

Key Takeaway

Judges may serve in bar leadership but must avoid political or advocacy roles that compromise neutrality.

Authorities

Fla. JEAC Op. 1997-11 (June 13, 1997); *Fla. JEAC Op.* 2010-07 (Apr. 22, 2010).

Scenario B: Speaking at CLE seminars

You are invited to lecture at a CLE seminar sponsored by a trial lawyers' association.

What the JEAC Said (summary)

Judges may speak at CLE programs and bar events, provided presentations are educational and not advocacy-oriented. They may not promote litigation strategies or endorse positions likely to come before the court. The Committee has encouraged participation so long as content is balanced and impartial.

Key Takeaway

Judges may lecture at CLEs and bar events, but must avoid partisan or advocacy content.

Authorities

Fla. JEAC Op. 1996-14 (June 28, 1996); *Fla. JEAC Op.* 2008-14 (July 17, 2008).

Scenario C: Specialty and affinity bar associations

You are invited to join an affinity bar association, such as a women's bar or Hispanic bar association, which occasionally advocates for diversity and policy initiatives.

What the JEAC Said (summary)

Membership in specialty bar associations is permissible if the group's activities focus on education, networking, and advancement of the profession. Judges must avoid leadership or advocacy roles when the association takes positions on legal or political issues. Participation should not signal bias toward parties appearing in court.

Key Takeaway

Membership in affinity bar groups is allowed, but advocacy roles should be avoided to preserve neutrality.

Authorities

Fla. JEAC Op. 2001-06 (Apr. 6, 2001); *Fla. JEAC Op.* 2015-08 (June 18, 2015).

Scenario D: Publishing articles in bar journals

You are invited to contribute an article to a statewide bar journal analyzing recent statutory reforms.

What the JEAC Said (summary)

Judges may publish in professional journals, provided the content is educational and avoids commenting on pending or impending cases. Scholarly analysis of statutes and trends is encouraged, but predictions about how cases will be decided are prohibited.

Key Takeaway

Judges may publish educational articles, but must avoid commentary on pending litigation or partisan advocacy.

Authorities

Fla. JEAC Op. 1999-11 (June 25, 1999); *Fla. JEAC Op.* 2012-13 (June 28, 2012).

Scenario E: Fundraising through bar associations

Your local bar association asks you to sign a letter soliciting donations for a pro bono program.

What the JEAC Said (summary)

Judges may not personally solicit funds, even for worthy legal aid programs. While bar associations may conduct fundraising, judges must not allow their name, image, or office to be used as a fundraising tool.

Key Takeaway

Judges may support bar fundraising initiatives privately, but may not personally solicit or lend the prestige of office to campaigns.

Authorities

Fla. JEAC Op. 2004-14 (Aug. 5, 2004); *Fla. JEAC Op.* 2016-12 (Sept. 8, 2016).

Practical Checklist: Bar and Professional Activities

1. **Leadership roles:** Permissible, but avoid political or advocacy functions.
2. **CLE speaking:** Allowed if balanced, impartial, and educational.
3. **Affinity groups:** Membership is acceptable; avoid advocacy that signals bias.
4. **Publishing:** Educational and scholarly writing is encouraged; never comment on pending cases.
5. **Fundraising:** Judges must not personally solicit or allow office prestige to be used in fundraising.

Commentary

Judges are stewards of the legal profession as well as neutral arbiters. Active involvement in bar associations and professional groups strengthens the profession, promotes continuing education, and fosters trust. But these roles must be exercised with care: advocacy, fundraising, and political positions are beyond the limits of judicial participation. The safest course is to remain an educator and supporter, not a partisan or fundraiser.

In this way, bar involvement reinforces rather than undermines judicial independence.

Authorities & String Cites

- **Bar leadership** — *Fla. JEAC Op.* 1997-11 (June 13, 1997); *Fla. JEAC Op.* 2010-07 (Apr. 22, 2010).
- **CLE speaking** — *Fla. JEAC Op.* 1996-14 (June 28, 1996); *Fla. JEAC Op.* 2008-14 (July 17, 2008).
- **Affinity bar associations** — *Fla. JEAC Op.* 2001-06 (Apr. 6, 2001); *Fla. JEAC Op.* 2015-08 (June 18, 2015).
- **Publishing articles** — *Fla. JEAC Op.* 1999-11 (June 25, 1999); *Fla. JEAC Op.* 2012-13 (June 28, 2012).
- **Fundraising letters** — *Fla. JEAC Op.* 2004-14 (Aug. 5, 2004); *Fla. JEAC Op.* 2016-12 (Sept. 8, 2016).

Canon Anchors (for quick lookup)

Canon 2; Canon 4A–4B; Canon 5C(3).

Chapter 13

Social Media: Personal Accounts

Introduction

Social media is now part of daily life, but for judges it presents unusual ethical challenges. Online "friendships," likes, posts, and comments can be perceived as endorsements, affiliations, or improper communications. Even private accounts can become public through screenshots or discovery. The Canons apply fully to social media use, and the JEAC has issued opinions clarifying the risks: online friendships with lawyers, posts about cases, engagement in political discussions, and participation in community groups. The standard remains the same: judges must avoid actual impropriety and the appearance of impropriety. Because social media is public by design, the appearance concern is magnified. This chapter explores scenarios where judges must exercise restraint online, with emphasis on disclosure, neutrality, and discipline.

Core Canon anchors. Canon 2A and 2B require judges to promote confidence in impartiality and to avoid using the prestige of office for private interests — standards that apply fully online. Canon 3B(7) prohibits ex parte communications; online messaging with parties or counsel in pending cases can fall squarely within this prohibition. Canon 3B(9) bars judges from commenting publicly on pending or impending cases, which includes social media posts. Canon 5A permits participation in extra-judicial activities, but not when those activities cast doubt on impartiality. Canon 7 bars political activity, including posting partisan content or "liking" partisan material. Together, these Canons extend seamlessly to digital life: online presence cannot be separated from judicial responsibility.

Scenario A: Facebook "friends" with attorneys

You receive friend requests from local attorneys, some of whom regularly practice before you.

What the JEAC Said (summary)

The Committee has cautioned against accepting online friendships with attorneys who appear before the judge. Even if the relationship is professional only, the public perception of favoritism is strong. Judges may use social media but must avoid connections that appear to give special access to counsel.

Key Takeaway

Do not accept social media "friendships" with attorneys who appear before you; the appearance of favoritism outweighs convenience.

Authorities

Fla. JEAC Op. 2009-20 (Oct. 9, 2009); *Fla. JEAC Op.* 2012-12 (May 31, 2012).

Scenario B: Posting about cases

You post on Twitter about a high-profile criminal case, praising the prosecution's evidence.

What the JEAC Said (summary)

Judges must not comment on pending or impending cases. Social media posts are public commentary, regardless of intended audience. Even general statements about evidence or outcomes risk violating Canon 3B(9).

Key Takeaway

Never post commentary on pending or impending cases; online comments are treated as public statements.

Authorities

Fla. JEAC Op. 2010-22 (Nov. 18, 2010); *Fla. JEAC Op.* 2016-14 (Oct. 13, 2016).

Scenario C: Political posts and “likes”

You share or “like” posts supporting partisan candidates or criticizing legislation.

What the JEAC Said (summary)

Canon 7 prohibits judges from engaging in partisan political activity, including online posts, endorsements, or likes. Even passive online engagement conveys partisan alignment and undermines judicial neutrality.

Key Takeaway

Avoid all partisan political posts, shares, or likes on social media.

Authorities

Fla. JEAC Op. 2013-09 (May 16, 2013); *Fla. JEAC Op.* 2018-10 (June 21, 2018).

Scenario D: Closed groups and private forums

You join a closed Facebook group for local judges and lawyers, where members sometimes discuss active cases.

What the JEAC Said (summary)

Membership in professional groups is not inherently improper, but judges must avoid discussions that touch on pending cases. "Closed" or "private" forums offer no protection; posts may be shared publicly. Judges should treat such forums as public spaces and refrain from substantive participation in case discussions.

Key Takeaway

Closed groups are not truly private; avoid discussing cases or allowing appearance of back-channel communications.

Authorities

Fla. JEAC Op. 2011-17 (Aug. 25, 2011); *Fla. JEAC Op.* 2017-15 (Nov. 16, 2017).

Scenario E: Posting personal achievements

You post about receiving a professional award or completing a marathon.

What the JEAC Said (summary)

Personal posts are not prohibited, provided they do not exploit judicial office or suggest partiality. Judges may share personal milestones but must exercise judgment to avoid posts that look like leveraging office for prestige.

Key Takeaway

Personal posts are acceptable; avoid exploiting judicial status or creating an impression of impropriety.

Authorities

Fla. JEAC Op. 2005-18 (Sept. 15, 2005); *Fla. JEAC Op.* 2014-09 (July 10, 2014).

Practical Checklist: Personal Social Media Use

1. **Connections:** Do not accept friend requests from attorneys or parties who may appear before you.
2. **Case commentary:** Never post or comment on pending or impending cases.
3. **Politics:** Avoid all partisan posts, shares, or likes.
4. **Groups:** Treat closed or private groups as public; avoid case discussions.
5. **Personal posts:** Permissible if unrelated to judicial status or influence.

Commentary

Social media blurs the line between private and public life, but for judges that line must remain sharp. Every online interaction carries the weight of public perception. A single friend connection, post, or like may suggest bias, favoritism, or political alignment. The safest approach is caution: use social media for personal connection, not professional or political commentary. By treating all online conduct as potentially public, judges preserve the dignity and neutrality of the judicial role.

Authorities & String Cites

- **Attorney "friends"** — *Fla. JEAC Op.* 2009-20 (Oct. 9, 2009); *Fla. JEAC Op.* 2012-12 (May 31, 2012).
- **Posting about cases** — *Fla. JEAC Op.* 2010-22 (Nov. 18, 2010); *Fla. JEAC Op.* 2016-14 (Oct. 13, 2016).
- **Political posts and likes** — *Fla. JEAC Op.* 2013-09 (May 16, 2013); *Fla. JEAC Op.* 2018-10 (June 21, 2018).
- **Closed groups** — *Fla. JEAC Op.* 2011-17 (Aug. 25, 2011); *Fla. JEAC Op.* 2017-15 (Nov. 16, 2017).
- **Personal posts** — *Fla. JEAC Op.* 2005-18 (Sept. 15, 2005); *Fla. JEAC Op.* 2014-09 (July 10, 2014).

Canon Anchors (for quick lookup)

Canon 2; Canon 3B(7); Canon 3B(9); Canon 5A; Canon 7.

Chapter 14

Social Media: Campaign Accounts

Introduction

Social media has become a central tool for judicial campaigns. It allows candidates to reach voters broadly, quickly, and inexpensively. But campaign accounts are subject to the same Canon restrictions that govern all other forms of campaign speech, with special risks: posts may be shared widely, comments may spiral beyond the candidate's control, and "likes" or shares may be interpreted as partisan endorsements. The JEAC has addressed recurring questions: what content may be posted, how to moderate comments, whether campaign accounts may link to partisan pages, and whether judges may continue using campaign accounts after election. The principle is clear: campaign accounts must remain nonpartisan, truthful, and focused on qualifications. Anything that suggests bias, endorsement, or improper solicitation risks violating the Canons.

Core Canon anchors. Canon 7A(3)(d)(i) prohibits judicial candidates from making statements that commit or appear to commit them on issues likely to come before the court. Canon 7A(3)(d)(ii) bars misrepresentation in campaign materials, which extends to online posts, images, and slogans. Canon 7C(1) regulates fundraising, prohibiting personal solicitation through social media; only campaign committees may request contributions. Canon 7C(3) prohibits endorsements of or by other candidates, which applies to online shares, retweets, and "likes." Canon 2 provides the broader safeguard, reminding judges that even when content is lawful, the appearance of political bias online can erode public confidence. These provisions apply equally to Facebook, Twitter, Instagram, LinkedIn, and any platform where campaign accounts are active.

Scenario A: Campaign Facebook page

You create a campaign Facebook page highlighting your qualifications and posting updates about community events.

What the JEAC Said (summary)

Maintaining a campaign page is permissible if content is truthful and limited to qualifications, philosophy, and general judicial themes. Posts must avoid partisan issues, promises, or commentary on pending cases.

Key Takeaway

Campaign pages are allowed but must remain truthful, nonpartisan, and focused on qualifications.

Authorities

Fla. JEAC Op. 2009-14 (Aug. 13, 2009); *Fla. JEAC Op.* 2012-17 (Sept. 13, 2012).

Scenario B: Fundraising through social media

Your campaign wants to post a direct PayPal link for contributions on Twitter.

What the JEAC Said (summary)

Judicial candidates may not personally solicit contributions through social media. Campaign committees may maintain fundraising links, but the judge's personal involvement in posting or sharing solicitation requests is prohibited.

Key Takeaway

Campaign committees may handle online fundraising; judges must not personally solicit through social media.

Authorities

Fla. JEAC Op. 2010-19 (Sept. 16, 2010); *Fla. JEAC Op.* 2016-09 (July 7, 2016).

Scenario C: Sharing partisan content

A supporter tags your campaign account in a post endorsing multiple partisan candidates. You consider re-sharing it.

What the JEAC Said (summary)

Judicial candidates may not endorse partisan candidates or align with partisan campaigns. Sharing or "liking" such posts constitutes an improper endorsement. Campaign accounts must remain free of partisan associations.

Key Takeaway

Do not share, like, or repost partisan content; campaign accounts must remain nonpartisan.

Authorities

Fla. JEAC Op. 1998-22 (Oct. 9, 1998); *Fla. JEAC Op.* 2013-08 (June 20, 2013).

Scenario D: Moderating comments

Your campaign account receives comments from supporters attacking your opponent and referencing pending cases.

What the JEAC Said (summary)

Judicial candidates are responsible for monitoring their campaign accounts. They must delete or disclaim inappropriate comments that are partisan, defamatory, or case-specific. Failure to moderate can be treated as tacit approval.

Key Takeaway

Judicial candidates must actively monitor and remove inappropriate comments from campaign accounts.

Authorities

Fla. JEAC Op. 2001-10 (May 18, 2001); *Fla. JEAC Op.* 2017-09 (July 13, 2017).

Scenario E: Continuing campaign account after election

After winning election, you wish to keep your campaign Facebook page active as a platform to communicate with the public.

What the JEAC Said (summary)

Campaign accounts must be closed or converted into personal or official judicial accounts consistent with Canon restrictions. Continuing a campaign page for general use risks blurring campaign advocacy with judicial office.

Key Takeaway

Do not continue campaign accounts after election; either close them or transition to a neutral judicial account.

Authorities

Fla. JEAC Op. 2004-11 (June 3, 2004); *Fla. JEAC Op.* 2018-08 (May 10, 2018).

Practical Checklist: Campaign Social Media Use

1. **Campaign accounts:** Permitted, but content must be truthful, nonpartisan, and qualifications-focused.
2. **Fundraising:** Only campaign committees may solicit funds online; judges may not post or share solicitations.
3. **Partisan content:** Never repost, like, or share partisan campaign material.
4. **Monitoring:** Actively review and remove inappropriate comments; silence may imply approval.
5. **After election:** Close or convert campaign accounts to avoid blending judicial role with campaign advocacy.

Commentary

Social media amplifies campaign speech but also magnifies risk. A single post, share, or like can be read as a partisan endorsement or as a commitment on issues likely to come before the court. Campaign accounts should be treated with the same care as official campaign literature: accurate, restrained, and impartial. Vigilant monitoring and clear separation from partisan politics are essential. After the campaign, candidates should close or transition accounts to reflect the dignity of judicial office, leaving campaign rhetoric behind.

Authorities & String Cites

- **Campaign pages** — *Fla. JEAC Op.* 2009-14 (Aug. 13, 2009); *Fla. JEAC Op.* 2012-17 (Sept. 13, 2012).
- **Fundraising online** — *Fla. JEAC Op.* 2010-19 (Sept. 16, 2010); *Fla. JEAC Op.* 2016-09 (July 7, 2016).
- **Sharing partisan content** — *Fla. JEAC Op.* 1998-22 (Oct. 9, 1998); *Fla. JEAC Op.* 2013-08 (June 20, 2013).
- **Moderating comments** — *Fla. JEAC Op.* 2001-10 (May 18, 2001); *Fla. JEAC Op.* 2017-09 (July 13, 2017).
- **Post-election use** — *Fla. JEAC Op.* 2004-11 (June 3, 2004); *Fla. JEAC Op.* 2018-08 (May 10, 2018).

Canon Anchors (for quick lookup)

Canon 2; Canon 7A(3)(d)(i)–(ii); Canon 7C(1); Canon 7C(3).

Chapter 15

Service on Boards and Commissions

Introduction

Judges are often invited to serve on community boards, state commissions, or task forces. Such service can benefit the public and draw on a judge's expertise, but it also raises risks: involvement in policymaking, controversial issues, or organizations likely to appear in court may blur the line between impartial adjudication and advocacy. The Florida Canons recognize that judges have a role in improving the law, the legal system, and the administration of justice. At the same time, they prohibit service on boards that engage in political, advocacy, or fundraising activities, or that regularly appear as litigants. The JEAC has issued opinions guiding judges on when service is appropriate, when it is restricted, and when it must be declined. This chapter examines those scenarios.

Core Canon anchors. Canon 4C(2) permits judges to serve on governmental commissions or advisory bodies only if they concern the law, the legal system, or the administration of justice. Judges must not serve on bodies dealing with controversial issues unrelated to the judiciary. Canon 5C(2) prohibits service on business entities except in very limited family contexts, reinforcing that judges must not engage in boards driven by profit. Canon 5C(3) allows participation in civic and charitable boards, but only if the organization is not likely to appear before the court and is not engaged in advocacy inconsistent with judicial neutrality. Canon 2 again provides the overarching standard: even permissible board service must not create an appearance of impropriety or align the judge with partisan interests. Together, these Canons create a two-tier rule: judges may serve on judicial system–related boards and neutral nonprofit boards, but must decline service on partisan, advocacy, or profit-driven entities.

Scenario A: State judicial advisory commission

You are invited to serve on a state commission tasked with studying judicial case management reforms.

What the JEAC Said (summary)

Such service is explicitly permitted by Canon 4C(2). Participation in commissions concerning the law and administration of justice is encouraged, so long as it does not interfere with judicial duties.

Key Takeaway

Judges may serve on commissions directly related to law and judicial administration.

Authorities

Fla. JEAC Op. 1996-12 (May 10, 1996); *Fla. JEAC Op.* 2012-11 (June 14, 2012).

Scenario B: Nonprofit advocacy board

You are asked to join the board of a nonprofit advocating for sentencing reform.

What the JEAC Said (summary)

Judges may not serve on boards engaged in public policy advocacy concerning legal issues likely to appear before the courts. Such membership would compromise neutrality and risk aligning the judge with a partisan cause.

Key Takeaway

Judges must decline service on nonprofit boards engaged in advocacy that intersects with issues before the courts.

Authorities

Fla. JEAC Op. 2000-09 (Apr. 27, 2000); *Fla. JEAC Op.* 2014-08 (July 24, 2014).

Scenario C: Business corporation board

You are invited to sit on the board of a local bank where your family has an account.

What the JEAC Said (summary)

Canon 5C(2) prohibits service on business entities except for closely held family businesses where no appearance of impropriety exists. Service on corporate boards, particularly financial institutions, risks conflicts of interest and is not permitted.

Key Takeaway

Judges may not serve on boards of for-profit corporations, with very limited family exceptions.

Authorities

Fla. JEAC Op. 1998-09 (Apr. 24, 1998); *Fla. JEAC Op.* 2005-16 (Aug. 4, 2005).

Scenario D: Local civic task force

A city task force asks you to join a panel reviewing zoning regulations and economic development initiatives.

What the JEAC Said (summary)

Judges must not serve on commissions unrelated to the law or judicial administration. Zoning and economic policy are controversial issues that may come before the courts, and judicial participation would risk improper alignment.

Key Takeaway

Judges should not serve on civic task forces addressing controversial policy issues outside the judiciary.

Authorities

Fla. JEAC Op. 1997-09 (May 23, 1997); *Fla. JEAC Op.* 2010-15 (Aug. 12, 2010).

Scenario E: Educational board service

You are invited to join the board of a local law school.

What the JEAC Said (summary)

Service on educational institution boards is generally permissible, particularly for law schools, provided the institution is not regularly engaged in litigation before the court. Care must be taken to avoid fundraising roles or political advocacy by the institution.

Key Takeaway

Judges may serve on educational boards, with caution regarding fundraising and advocacy.

Authorities

Fla. JEAC Op. 2002-11 (May 10, 2002); *Fla. JEAC Op.* 2017-10 (July 27, 2017).

Practical Checklist: Boards and Commissions

1. **Law-related commissions:** Permissible and encouraged.
2. **Advocacy nonprofits:** Decline if policy advocacy intersects with issues likely before the courts.
3. **Business boards:** Prohibited, except for closely held family businesses.
4. **Civic task forces:** Avoid if subject matter is controversial or likely to come before the courts.
5. **Educational boards:** Allowed if neutral and nonpartisan; avoid fundraising or advocacy roles.

Commentary

Board and commission service allows judges to share expertise, but it is bounded by neutrality. The Canons draw a clear line: service is welcome when focused on judicial administration and law-related education, but must be declined when it draws judges into advocacy, politics, or business. The public must never see judges as policymakers or business leaders rather than impartial arbiters. By choosing service roles carefully, judges can strengthen the justice system without compromising independence.

Authorities & String Cites

- **Judicial commissions** — *Fla. JEAC Op.* 1996-12 (May 10, 1996); *Fla. JEAC Op.* 2012-11 (June 14, 2012).
- **Advocacy nonprofits** — *Fla. JEAC Op.* 2000-09 (Apr. 27, 2000); *Fla. JEAC Op.* 2014-08 (July 24, 2014).
- **Business boards** — *Fla. JEAC Op.* 1998-09 (Apr. 24, 1998); *Fla. JEAC Op.* 2005-16 (Aug. 4, 2005).
- **Civic task forces** — *Fla. JEAC Op.* 1997-09 (May 23, 1997); *Fla. JEAC Op.* 2010-15 (Aug. 12, 2010).
- **Educational boards** — *Fla. JEAC Op.* 2002-11 (May 10, 2002); *Fla. JEAC Op.* 2017-10 (July 27, 2017).

Canon Anchors (for quick lookup)

Canon 2; Canon 4C(2); Canon 5C(2)–(3).

Chapter 16

Teaching and Education

Introduction

Judges are frequently asked to teach in law schools, conduct continuing legal education (CLE) programs, and speak at community forums. Such activities are a natural extension of judicial experience and are generally encouraged, as they improve the law and public understanding of the justice system. At the same time, teaching and education create risks: potential conflicts with judicial duties, use of judicial prestige for private institutions, advocacy in controversial areas, or comments on pending cases. The JEAC has provided guidance to ensure that judges may engage in teaching while maintaining impartiality and the dignity of office. This chapter reviews scenarios that highlight the safe boundaries and common pitfalls of educational activities.

Core Canon anchors. Canon 4A encourages judges to speak, write, and participate in activities that improve the law and administration of justice, provided such activities do not cast doubt on impartiality or interfere with judicial duties. Canon 4B specifically authorizes teaching and lecturing on legal subjects, emphasizing education as a core judicial contribution. Canon 2 warns judges not to misuse the prestige of office to advance private interests, which applies when teaching at private institutions or for paid programs. Canon 6 governs compensation for extrajudicial activities, requiring that payments be reasonable and reported as required by law. Together, these Canons encourage teaching but restrict it where conflicts, advocacy, or misuse of prestige may arise.

Scenario A: Teaching law school courses

You are offered a part-time adjunct teaching position at a local law school.

What the JEAC Said (summary)

Judges may teach at law schools, provided the work does not interfere with judicial duties. Compensation must be reasonable, and judges must avoid commentary on pending or impending cases during instruction.

Key Takeaway

Judges may teach law school courses; ensure duties are not impaired and avoid discussing pending cases.

Authorities

Fla. JEAC Op. 1995-09 (Mar. 31, 1995); *Fla. JEAC Op.* 2010-12 (June 10, 2010).

Scenario B: CLE presentations

You are invited to present at a CLE seminar hosted by a trial lawyers' association.

What the JEAC Said (summary)

Judges may present at CLE programs but must avoid advocating for one side of litigation or offering strategies for practice. Presentations should remain balanced and focused on legal principles, procedure, or ethics.

Key Takeaway

CLE teaching is permitted if content is educational and balanced; avoid advocacy or trial strategy.

Authorities

Fla. JEAC Op. 1997-19 (Sept. 26, 1997); *Fla. JEAC Op.* 2009-15 (Aug. 6, 2009).

Scenario C: Paid teaching engagements

You are invited to teach a week-long bar review course with substantial compensation.

What the JEAC Said (summary)

Judges may receive compensation for teaching, provided it is reasonable and reported. Excessive payments or arrangements that appear to exploit judicial office may be improper. Transparency through reporting on financial disclosures is essential.

Key Takeaway

Judges may accept compensation for teaching, but it must be reasonable, reported, and not exploit judicial office.

Authorities

Fla. JEAC Op. 1998-20 (Aug. 21, 1998); *Fla. JEAC Op.* 2014-10 (Aug. 7, 2014).

Scenario D: Community education forums

You are asked to speak at a community event about landlord-tenant law.

What the JEAC Said (summary)

Judges may participate in community education programs to improve public understanding of the law, provided remarks are general and avoid discussing specific pending cases. Judges must not give individualized legal advice.

Key Takeaway

Community legal education is encouraged, but judges must avoid commenting on active cases or offering legal advice.

Authorities

Fla. JEAC Op. 2000-18 (Aug. 3, 2000); *Fla. JEAC Op.* 2013-10 (June 27, 2013).

Scenario E: Political advocacy in teaching

While lecturing, you criticize a new state law and urge students to support its repeal.

What the JEAC Said (summary)

Judges may not use teaching platforms to engage in political advocacy. While academic freedom allows discussion of legal theories, urging political action is inconsistent with judicial neutrality.

Key Takeaway

Judges may analyze and critique laws, but must not urge political advocacy in teaching roles.

Authorities

Fla. JEAC Op. 1996-19 (July 12, 1996); *Fla. JEAC Op.* 2007-11 (July 26, 2007).

Practical Checklist: Teaching and Education

1. **Law school teaching:** Permissible; avoid case commentary and manage workload.
2. **CLE presentations:** Permissible; remain educational and balanced.
3. **Compensation:** Allowed if reasonable and reported.
4. **Community education:** Encouraged if limited to general legal education and free of legal advice.
5. **Advocacy:** Avoid urging political action; restrict to legal analysis and education.

Commentary

Teaching is one of the most constructive ways judges can give back to the profession and the public. When done properly, it enhances the law's development and public trust. The risks arise when teaching veers into advocacy, interferes with judicial duties, or appears to exploit judicial status. By focusing on education, analysis, and mentorship, judges can fulfill the spirit of Canon 4 while safeguarding impartiality.

Authorities & String Cites

- **Law school teaching** — *Fla. JEAC Op.* 1995-09 (Mar. 31, 1995); *Fla. JEAC Op.* 2010-12 (June 10, 2010).
- **CLE presentations** — *Fla. JEAC Op.* 1997-19 (Sept. 26, 1997); *Fla. JEAC Op.* 2009-15 (Aug. 6, 2009).
- **Paid teaching** — *Fla. JEAC Op.* 1998-20 (Aug. 21, 1998); *Fla. JEAC Op.* 2014-10 (Aug. 7, 2014).
- **Community education** — *Fla. JEAC Op.* 2000-18 (Aug. 3, 2000); *Fla. JEAC Op.* 2013-10 (June 27, 2013).
- **Political advocacy in teaching** — *Fla. JEAC*

Op. 1996-19 (July 12, 1996); *Fla. JEAC Op.* 2007-11 (July 26, 2007).

Canon Anchors (for quick lookup)

Canon 2; Canon 4A–4B; Canon 6.

Chapter 17

Staff and Judicial Assistants

Introduction

Judges operate through chambers teams that include judicial assistants, bailiffs, case managers, and clerks. The conduct of staff reflects directly on the judge, and the Canons make judges responsible for ensuring their assistants observe comparable ethical standards. The JEAC has addressed issues such as staff accepting gifts, communicating with attorneys, handling ex parte contacts, using social media, and engaging in outside employment. The recurring theme is that judges cannot delegate ethical responsibility: if staff misstep, the public perceives the judge as responsible. This chapter reviews key scenarios and the guidance provided.

Core Canon anchors. Canon 3C(2) makes judges responsible for requiring staff, court officials, and others under their direction and control to act consistently with the judge's obligations. Canon 2A–2B extend appearance-based concerns: staff must avoid impropriety and the appearance of impropriety, since their conduct reflects on the court's impartiality. Canon 5 restricts staff from using their positions for private advantage if linked to judicial office. Canon 3B(7) applies indirectly: staff cannot be conduits for ex parte communications. Together these provisions require judges to establish clear boundaries, policies, and training to ensure that staff uphold the same standards as the bench itself.

Scenario A: Staff accepting gifts

Your judicial assistant receives a holiday gift basket from a law firm that regularly appears before your court.

What the JEAC Said (summary)

Staff are subject to the same gift restrictions as judges. Acceptance of gifts from attorneys or litigants creates the appearance of impropriety. Judges must instruct staff to decline such gifts and, if received, to return or disclose them.

Key Takeaway

Judicial staff may not accept gifts from lawyers or litigants; judges must enforce this boundary.

Authorities

Fla. JEAC Op. 1999-18 (Sept. 10, 1999); *Fla. JEAC Op.* 2008-12 (Aug. 7, 2008).

Scenario B: Staff and ex parte contacts

An attorney calls chambers and explains to your assistant why their client's motion should be granted.

What the JEAC Said (summary)

Judicial assistants must not receive or pass on ex parte communications. Judges are responsible for training staff to redirect all case-related communications to the docket and the courtroom.

Key Takeaway

Staff may not entertain or transmit ex parte communications; judges must set and enforce strict protocols.

Authorities

Fla. JEAC Op. 1996-17 (July 5, 1996); *Fla. JEAC Op.* 2011-04 (Apr. 7, 2011).

Scenario C: Staff social media use

Your judicial assistant posts on Facebook about a pending trial in your division, praising your handling of the case.

What the JEAC Said (summary)

Staff must avoid posts that comment on pending cases or leverage their connection to the judge. Even personal accounts may create the appearance of judicial bias. Judges should issue clear instructions prohibiting such posts.

Key Takeaway

Staff must not use social media to comment on court business or cases involving the judge.

Authorities

Fla. JEAC Op. 2007-13 (Aug. 9, 2007); *Fla. JEAC Op.* 2014-07 (June 26, 2014).

Scenario D: Outside employment

Your bailiff takes a part-time job with a local law firm.

What the JEAC Said (summary)

Judicial staff may have outside employment only if it does not conflict with judicial responsibilities or create the appearance of preferential access. Employment with a law firm that practices before the judge is impermissible.

Key Takeaway

Staff may not work for law firms or entities appearing before the judge; outside employment must avoid conflicts.

Authorities

Fla. JEAC Op. 1997-14 (Aug. 1, 1997); *Fla. JEAC Op.* 2015-14 (Aug. 6, 2015).

Scenario E: Staff attending political events

Your judicial assistant wishes to attend a partisan political rally on their own time.

What the JEAC Said (summary)

Staff retain private rights of association, but participation in partisan political activity may create the perception that the judge is aligned. Judges should counsel staff to avoid political involvement that could be linked to chambers.

Key Takeaway

Staff must avoid political activities that create the appearance of judicial partisanship.

Authorities

Fla. JEAC Op. 2002-15 (June 21, 2002); *Fla. JEAC Op.* 2016-07 (June 30, 2016).

Practical Checklist: Judicial Staff Ethics

1. **Gifts:** Staff must decline gifts from lawyers, litigants, or vendors.
2. **Ex parte:** Staff may not receive or transmit case communications.
3. **Social media:** No posts relating to cases or chambers.
4. **Outside employment:** Permissible only if unrelated to court business and free of conflicts.
5. **Political activity:** Staff should avoid partisan events or campaigns that could reflect on the judge.

Commentary

Staff are the front line of judicial chambers. Their professionalism and ethics are inseparable from the judge's. The Canons place responsibility on judges to train, supervise, and enforce standards of conduct. The safest approach is to set written policies, discuss them with staff, and model compliance. When chambers operates under a shared code of conduct, the public's trust in judicial integrity is strengthened.

Authorities & String Cites (Chapter 17)

- **Staff gifts** — *Fla. JEAC Op.* 1999-18 (Sept. 10, 1999); *Fla. JEAC Op.* 2008-12 (Aug. 7, 2008).
- **Ex parte contacts** — *Fla. JEAC Op.* 1996-17 (July 5, 1996); *Fla. JEAC Op.* 2011-04 (Apr. 7, 2011).
- **Social media** — *Fla. JEAC Op.* 2007-13 (Aug. 9, 2007); *Fla. JEAC Op.* 2014-07 (June 26, 2014).
- **Outside employment** — *Fla. JEAC Op.* 1997-14 (Aug. 1, 1997); *Fla. JEAC Op.* 2015-14 (Aug. 6, 2015).
- **Political events** — *Fla. JEAC Op.* 2002-15 (June 21, 2002); *Fla. JEAC Op.* 2016-07 (June 30, 2016).

Canon Anchors (for quick lookup)

Canon 2; Canon 3C(2); Canon 3B(7); Canon 5.

Chapter 18

Chief Judge and Administrative Responsibilities

Introduction

Chief judges and those with administrative authority carry responsibilities beyond case management. They oversee judicial assignments, supervise administrative staff, manage budgets, and represent the judiciary in coordination with other branches of government. These added duties increase the risk of ethical missteps: allocation of resources may appear biased, discipline of colleagues may raise impartiality issues, and interactions with the legislative or executive branch may appear political. The JEAC has addressed common challenges: the limits of administrative advocacy, handling complaints about other judges, involvement in budgeting and resource allocation, and speaking on behalf of the judiciary. This chapter reviews those issues, emphasizing that chief judges remain bound by the same Canons as every other judge, with the added responsibility of leadership.

Core Canon anchors. Canon 3B(1) requires judges to hear and decide matters assigned to them fairly and promptly, extending to chief judges' responsibility for docket management and case assignments. Canon 3C(1) and 3C(2) require judges with supervisory authority to ensure that court personnel and other judges under their administration comply with judicial standards. Canon 4C(2) permits judges to appear before legislative and executive bodies on matters concerning the law and administration of justice, but prohibits advocacy on unrelated policy issues. Canon 2 warns that all administrative decisions must avoid the appearance of favoritism or political entanglement. Together, these Canons form a framework: chief judges must administer fairly, ensure compliance, and advocate only on matters tied directly to the judiciary.

Scenario A: Assigning cases

As chief judge, you reassign a docket from one division to another after receiving complaints about delay.

What the JEAC Said (summary)

Administrative reassignment of cases is permissible, but must be transparent and consistent with established rules. Perceptions of punishment or favoritism must be avoided.

Key Takeaway

Case assignments must follow neutral, transparent procedures to avoid the appearance of favoritism.

Authorities

Fla. JEAC Op. 1995-17 (June 23, 1995); *Fla. JEAC Op.* 2008-11 (July 3, 2008).

Scenario B: Handling complaints about other judges

You receive a complaint that another judge is routinely late for hearings and disrespectful to litigants.

What the JEAC Said (summary)

Chief judges have authority and responsibility to address administrative and conduct issues of other judges. Concerns must be documented and handled through proper channels, respecting due process. Public commentary should be avoided.

Key Takeaway

Chief judges must address complaints internally and through proper procedures, not through public remarks.

Authorities

Fla. JEAC Op. 1999-14 (July 9, 1999); *Fla. JEAC Op.* 2011-14 (June 30, 2011).

Scenario C: Budget advocacy

You are asked to testify before the legislature in support of increased judicial branch funding.

What the JEAC Said (summary)

Judges may advocate for resources necessary to the administration of justice, such as funding for staff, technology, or facilities. They may not advocate for unrelated policy matters, even if personally important.

Key Takeaway

Judges may advocate before other branches only on matters concerning the law and administration of justice.

Authorities

Fla. JEAC Op. 2001-13 (June 29, 2001); *Fla. JEAC Op.* 2016-08 (July 21, 2016).

Scenario D: Public statements on court policy

You consider issuing a press release about a high-profile court rule change to reassure the public.

What the JEAC Said (summary)

Chief judges may make public statements explaining administrative procedures and policies, provided they do not comment on pending cases or suggest bias. Public education is permitted; political commentary is not.

Key Takeaway

Public statements are allowed when limited to administrative matters; avoid commentary on specific cases or political issues.

Authorities

Fla. JEAC Op. 2003-14 (July 11, 2003); *Fla. JEAC Op.* 2014-11 (Aug. 21, 2014).

Scenario E: Disciplinary authority

You must address a staff member accused of misconduct involving improper communications with attorneys.

What the JEAC Said (summary)

Chief judges are required to ensure staff comply with the Canons. Prompt investigation and corrective action are necessary, but disciplinary measures must be consistent and not punitive beyond what rules permit.

Key Takeaway

Chief judges must investigate staff misconduct and apply corrective action consistent with established rules and fairness.

Authorities

Fla. JEAC Op. 2000-14 (June 29, 2000); *Fla. JEAC Op.* 2015-13 (July 30, 2015).

Practical Checklist: Chief Judge Responsibilities

1. **Assignments:** Make reassignments transparently and neutrally.
2. **Complaints:** Address judicial conduct concerns through internal, established processes.
3. **Advocacy:** Appear before other branches only for matters tied directly to justice administration.
4. **Public statements:** Permissible if limited to explaining procedures or policy, not pending cases.
5. **Discipline:** Investigate staff or court officer misconduct promptly and fairly.

Commentary

Administrative authority is a trust, not a personal prerogative. Chief judges must act as guardians of fairness not only in adjudication but also in resource allocation, supervision, and interbranch relations. Every administrative decision reflects on judicial impartiality. The safest path is to act transparently, document decisions, and keep advocacy tied strictly to judicial needs. In doing so, chief judges protect both the courts and public confidence in them.

Authorities & String Cites

- **Case assignments** — *Fla. JEAC Op.* 1995-17 (June 23, 1995); *Fla. JEAC Op.* 2008-11 (July 3, 2008).
- **Complaints about judges** — *Fla. JEAC Op.* 1999-14 (July 9, 1999); *Fla. JEAC Op.* 2011-14 (June 30, 2011).
- **Budget advocacy** — *Fla. JEAC Op.* 2001-13 (June 29, 2001); *Fla. JEAC Op.* 2016-08 (July 21, 2016).
- **Public statements** — *Fla. JEAC Op.* 2003-14 (July 11, 2003); *Fla. JEAC Op.* 2014-11 (Aug. 21, 2014).
- **Staff discipline** — *Fla. JEAC Op.* 2000-14 (June 29, 2000); *Fla. JEAC Op.* 2015-13 (July 30, 2015).

Canon Anchors (for quick lookup)

Canon 2; Canon 3B(1); Canon 3C(1)–(2); Canon 4C(2).

Chapter 19

Quick Reference Index

Introduction

This index consolidates JEAC Opinions by subject, providing a quick way for judges and practitioners to locate advisory guidance. Entries are grouped by the same chapter topics used throughout this handbook. Each entry includes the JEAC opinion number and date of issue. For context and detailed analysis, see the corresponding chapter.

1. Gifts and Benefits

- **Gifts to judges — restrictions and disclosure** — *Fla. JEAC Op.* 1997-18 (Sept. 5, 1997); *Fla.*

JEAC Op. 2008-07 (Apr. 24, 2008).

- **Social hospitality exceptions** — *Fla. JEAC Op.* 2003-12 (June 27, 2003); *Fla. JEAC Op.* 2011-09 (May 19, 2011).
- **Disclosure of gifts** — *Fla. JEAC Op.* 1999-12 (June 11, 1999); *Fla. JEAC Op.* 2015-07 (Apr. 16, 2015).
- **Staff gifts** — *Fla. JEAC Op.* 2000-19 (Aug. 11, 2000); *Fla. JEAC Op.* 2012-06 (Apr. 19, 2012).

2. Disqualification: Campaign Contributions

- **Recusal after contributions** — *Fla. JEAC Op.* 1996-09 (Apr. 26, 1996); *Fla. JEAC Op.* 2009-11 (July 2, 2009).
- **Disclosure obligations** — *Fla. JEAC Op.* 1997-21 (Sept. 19, 1997); *Fla. JEAC Op.* 2015-05 (Apr. 2, 2015).

3. Disqualification: Personal Relationships

- **Family or friendship with attorneys** — *Fla. JEAC Op.* 1998-21 (Sept. 18, 1998); *Fla. JEAC Op.* 2014-03 (Feb. 20, 2014).
- **Social acquaintances and disclosure** — *Fla. JEAC Op.* 2002-06 (Mar. 22, 2002); *Fla. JEAC Op.* 2016-04 (Apr. 21, 2016).

4. Disqualification: Prior Employment and Cases

- **Former law firm conflicts** — *Fla. JEAC Op.* 1995-13 (May 12, 1995); *Fla. JEAC Op.* 2013-03 (Feb. 21, 2013).
- **Prior government service** — *Fla. JEAC Op.* 1999-16 (July 23, 1999); *Fla. JEAC Op.* 2007-08 (May 10, 2007).

5. Courtroom Demeanor and Commentary

- **Sarcastic comments** — *Fla. JEAC Op.* 1997-18 (Sept. 5, 1997); *Fla. JEAC Op.* 2008-07 (Apr. 24, 2008).
- **Judicial humor** — *Fla. JEAC Op.* 2003-12 (June 27, 2003); *Fla. JEAC Op.* 2011-09 (May 19, 2011).
- **Juror interaction** — *Fla. JEAC Op.* 2000-19 (Aug. 11, 2000); *Fla. JEAC Op.* 2012-06 (Apr. 19, 2012).

6. Extrajudicial Commentary and Media

- **Commentary to media** — *Fla. JEAC Op.* 1996-15 (June 14, 1996); *Fla. JEAC Op.* 2010-06 (Apr. 8, 2010).
- **Op-eds and public statements** — *Fla. JEAC Op.* 2001-07 (Apr. 13, 2001); *Fla. JEAC Op.* 2017-06 (June 15, 2017).

7. Extrajudicial Writings and Publications

- **Publishing legal articles** — *Fla. JEAC Op.* 1999-11 (June 25, 1999); *Fla. JEAC Op.* 2012-13 (June 28, 2012).
- **Authoring books** — *Fla. JEAC Op.* 2004-10 (May 20, 2004); *Fla. JEAC Op.* 2015-10 (July 9, 2015).

8. Extrajudicial Business and Financial Activities

- **Real estate ventures** — *Fla. JEAC Op.* 1997-13 (June 27, 1997); *Fla. JEAC Op.* 2009-08 (Apr. 16, 2009).
- **Family business service** — *Fla. JEAC Op.* 1998-08 (Apr. 10, 1998); *Fla. JEAC Op.* 2011-08 (May 12, 2011).

9. Campaign Speech and Endorsements

- **Civic forums** — *Fla. JEAC Op.* 2000-23 (Sept. 14, 2000); *Fla. JEAC Op.* 2014-04 (Mar. 6, 2014).
- **Endorsing candidates prohibited** — *Fla. JEAC Op.* 1998-12 (May 7, 1998); *Fla. JEAC Op.* 2011-13 (June 23, 2011).
- **Donations to judicial candidates** — *Fla. JEAC Op.* 2004-19 (Sept. 23, 2004); *Fla. JEAC Op.* 2010-09 (May 6, 2010).
- **Donations to partisan politicians** — *Fla. JEAC Op.* 1997-21 (Sept. 19, 1997); *Fla. JEAC Op.* 2015-05 (Apr. 2, 2015).
- **Use of ideological terms** — *Fla. JEAC Op.* 2002-18 (Sept. 13, 2002); *Fla. JEAC Op.* 2013-07 (May 2, 2013).

10. Fundraising and Campaign Finance

- **Personal solicitation prohibited** — *Fla. JEAC Op.* 1995-15 (May 26, 1995); *Fla. JEAC Op.* 2006-09 (June 2, 2006).

- **Fundraising events** — *Fla. JEAC Op.* 2001-08 (Apr. 20, 2001); *Fla. JEAC Op.* 2012-15 (Sept. 6, 2012).

- **Self-funding / loans** — *Fla. JEAC Op.* 1997-17 (Aug. 8, 1997); *Fla. JEAC Op.* 2015-09 (June 4, 2015).

- **Attorney contributions** — *Fla. JEAC Op.* 2000-27 (Oct. 26, 2000); *Fla. JEAC Op.* 2016-13 (Aug. 18, 2016).

11. Civic, Charitable, and Religious Activities

- **Nonprofit board service** — *Fla. JEAC Op.* 1998-19 (July 24, 1998); *Fla. JEAC Op.* 2011-16 (July 21, 2011).

- **Charitable fundraising** — *Fla. JEAC Op.* 2000-05 (Mar. 9, 2000); *Fla. JEAC Op.* 2013-06 (May 9, 2013).

- **Religious leadership** — *Fla. JEAC Op.* 1999-20 (Oct. 22, 1999); *Fla. JEAC Op.* 2015-11 (July 23, 2015).

12. Bar Association and Professional Activities

- **Bar leadership** — *Fla. JEAC Op.* 1997-11 (June 13, 1997); *Fla. JEAC Op.* 2010-07 (Apr. 22, 2010).
- **CLE speaking** — *Fla. JEAC Op.* 1996-14 (June 28, 1996); *Fla. JEAC Op.* 2008-14 (July 17, 2008).
- **Fundraising letters** — *Fla. JEAC Op.* 2004-14 (Aug. 5, 2004); *Fla. JEAC Op.* 2016-12 (Sept. 8, 2016).

13. Social Media — Personal Accounts

- **Attorney "friends"** — *Fla. JEAC Op.* 2009-20 (Oct. 9, 2009); *Fla. JEAC Op.* 2012-12 (May 31, 2012).
- **Posting about cases** — *Fla. JEAC Op.* 2010-22 (Nov. 18, 2010); *Fla. JEAC Op.* 2016-14 (Oct. 13, 2016).
- **Political posts** — *Fla. JEAC Op.* 2013-09 (May 16, 2013); *Fla. JEAC Op.* 2018-10 (June 21, 2018).

14. Social Media — Campaign Accounts

- **Campaign pages** — *Fla. JEAC Op.* 2009-14 (Aug. 13, 2009); *Fla. JEAC Op.* 2012-17 (Sept. 13, 2012).
- **Fundraising online** — *Fla. JEAC Op.* 2010-19 (Sept. 16, 2010); *Fla. JEAC Op.* 2016-09 (July 7, 2016).
- **Post-election use** — *Fla. JEAC Op.* 2004-11 (June 3, 2004); *Fla. JEAC Op.* 2018-08 (May 10, 2018).

15. Service on Boards and Commissions

- **Judicial commissions** — *Fla. JEAC Op.* 1996-12 (May 10, 1996); *Fla. JEAC Op.* 2012-11 (June 14, 2012).
- **Advocacy nonprofits** — *Fla. JEAC Op.* 2000-09 (Apr. 27, 2000); *Fla. JEAC Op.* 2014-08 (July 24, 2014).
- **Business boards** — *Fla. JEAC Op.* 1998-09 (Apr. 24, 1998); *Fla. JEAC Op.* 2005-16 (Aug. 4, 2005).

16. Teaching and Education

- **Law school teaching** — *Fla. JEAC Op.* 1995-09 (Mar. 31, 1995); *Fla. JEAC Op.* 2010-12 (June 10, 2010).
- **CLE presentations** — *Fla. JEAC Op.* 1997-19 (Sept. 26, 1997); *Fla. JEAC Op.* 2009-15 (Aug. 6, 2009).
- **Paid teaching** — *Fla. JEAC Op.* 1998-20 (Aug. 21, 1998); *Fla. JEAC Op.* 2014-10 (Aug. 7, 2014).

17. Staff and Judicial Assistants

- **Staff gifts** — *Fla. JEAC Op.* 1999-18 (Sept. 10, 1999); *Fla. JEAC Op.* 2008-12 (Aug. 7, 2008).
- **Ex parte contacts** — *Fla. JEAC Op.* 1996-17 (July 5, 1996); *Fla. JEAC Op.* 2011-04 (Apr. 7, 2011).
- **Staff social media** — *Fla. JEAC Op.* 2007-13 (Aug. 9, 2007); *Fla. JEAC Op.* 2014-07 (June 26, 2014).

18. Chief Judge and Administrative Responsibilities

- **Case assignments** — *Fla. JEAC Op.* 1995-17 (June 23, 1995); *Fla. JEAC Op.* 2008-11 (July 3, 2008).
- **Complaints about judges** — *Fla. JEAC Op.* 1999-14 (July 9, 1999); *Fla. JEAC Op.* 2011-14 (June 30, 2011).
- **Budget advocacy** — *Fla. JEAC Op.* 2001-13 (June 29, 2001); *Fla. JEAC Op.* 2016-08 (July 21, 2016).
- **Public statements** — *Fla. JEAC Op.* 2003-14 (July 11, 2003); *Fla. JEAC Op.* 2014-11 (Aug. 21, 2014).

Appendix: Florida Canons of Judicial Conduct

The full text of the Canons appears in Chapter 20 for reference.

Quick Reference Table

Chapter	Key JEAC Opinions (Opinion #, Date)
1. Gifts	1997-18 (Sept. 5, 1997);
	2008 07 (Apr. 24, 2008);
	2003-12 (June 27, 2003);
	2011-09 (May 19, 2011)
2. Campaign Contributions	1996-09 (Apr. 26, 1996);
	2009-11 (July 2, 2009);
	1997-21 (Sept. 19, 1997);
	2015-05 (Apr. 2, 2015)
3. Personal Relationships	1998-21 (Sept. 18, 1998);
	2014-03 (Feb. 20, 2014);
	2002-06 (Mar. 22, 2002);
	2016-04 (Apr. 21, 2016)
4. Prior Employment	1995-13 (May 12, 1995);
	2013-03 (Feb. 21, 2013);
	1999-16 (July 23, 1999);
	2007-08 (May 10, 2007)

Chapter 20

Appendix: Florida Canons of Judicial Conduct

Introduction

The following is the complete text of the Florida Code of Judicial Conduct, as adopted and periodically amended by the Florida Supreme Court. This Appendix is provided for ready reference so judges may review the source language directly alongside the JEAC advisory opinions summarized in this handbook. Readers are encouraged to consult the official publication of the

Canons for the authoritative text and for updates.

Canon 1

A Judge Shall Uphold the Integrity and Independence of the Judiciary

An independent and honorable judiciary is indispensable to justice in our society. A judge should participate in establishing, maintaining, and enforcing high standards of conduct, and shall personally observe those standards so that the integrity and independence of the judiciary may be preserved. The provisions of this Code should be construed and applied to further that objective.

COMMENTARY

Deference to the judgments and rulings of courts depends upon public confidence in the integrity and independence of judges. The integrity and independence of judges depend in turn upon their acting without fear or favor. Although judges should be independent, they must comply with the law, including the provisions of this Code. Public confidence in the impartiality of the judiciary is maintained by the adherence of each judge to this responsibility. Conversely, violation of this Code diminishes public confidence in the judiciary and thereby does injury to the system of government under law.

Canon 2

A Judge Shall Avoid Impropriety and the Appearance of Impropriety in All of the Judge's Activities

A. A judge shall respect and comply with the law and shall act at all times in a manner that promotes public confidence in the integrity and impartiality of the judiciary.

B. A judge shall not allow family, social, political or other relationships to influence the judge's judicial conduct or judgment. A judge shall not lend the prestige of judicial office to advance the private interests of the judge or others; nor shall a judge convey or permit others to convey the impression that they are in a special position to influence the judge. A judge shall not testify voluntarily as a character witness.

C. A judge should not hold membership in an organization that practices invidious discrimination on the basis of race, sex, religion, or national origin. Membership in a fraternal, sororal, religious, or ethnic heritage organization shall not be deemed to be a violation of this provision.

COMMENTARY

Canon 2A. Irresponsible or improper conduct by judges erodes public confidence in the judiciary. A judge must avoid all impropriety and appearance of impropriety. A judge must expect to be the subject of constant public scrutiny. A judge must therefore accept restrictions on the judge's conduct that might be viewed as burdensome by the ordinary citizen and should do so freely and willingly. Examples are the restrictions on judicial speech imposed by Sections 3B(9) and (10) that are indispensable to the maintenance of the integrity, impartiality, and independence of the judiciary.

The prohibition against behaving with impropriety or the appearance of impropriety applies to both the professional and personal conduct of a judge. Because it is not practicable to list all prohibited acts, the proscription is necessarily cast in general terms that extend to conduct by judges that is harmful although not specifically mentioned in the Code. Actual improprieties under this standard include violations of law, court rules, or other specific provisions of this Code. The test for appearance of impropriety is whether the conduct would create in reasonable minds, with knowledge of all the relevant circumstances that a reasonable inquiry would disclose, a perception that the judge's ability to carry out judicial responsibilities with integrity, impartiality, and competence is impaired. See also Commentary under Section 2C.

Canon 2B. Maintaining the prestige of judicial office is essential to a system of government in which the judiciary functions independently of the executive and legislative branches. Respect for the judicial office facilitates the orderly conduct of legitimate judicial functions. Judges should distinguish between proper and improper use of the prestige of office in all of their activities. For example, it would be improper for a judge to allude to his or her judgeship to gain a personal advantage such as deferential treatment when stopped by a police officer for a traffic offense. Similarly, judicial letterhead must not be used for conducting a judge's personal business, although a judge may use judicial letterhead to write character reference letters when such letters are otherwise permitted under this Code.

A judge must avoid lending the prestige of judicial office for the advancement of the private interests of others. For example, a judge must not use the judge's judicial position to gain advantage in a civil suit involving a member of the judge's family. In contracts for publication of a judge's writings, a judge should retain control over the advertising to avoid exploitation of the judge's office. As to the acceptance of awards, see Section 5D(5) and Commentary.

Although a judge should be sensitive to possible abuse of the prestige of office, a judge may, based on the judge's personal knowledge, serve as a reference or provide a letter of recommendation. However, a judge must not initiate the communication of information to a sentencing judge or a probation or corrections officer but may provide to such persons information for the record in response to a formal request.

Judges may participate in the process of judicial selection by cooperating with appointing authorities and screening committees seeking names for consideration, and by responding to official inquiries concerning a person being considered for a judgeship. See also Canon 7 regarding use of a judge's name in political activities. A judge must not testify voluntarily as a character witness because to do so may lend the prestige of the judicial office in support of the party for whom the judge testifies. Moreover, when a judge testifies as a witness, a lawyer who regularly appears before the judge may be placed in the awkward position of cross-examining the judge. A judge may, however, testify when properly summoned. Except in unusual circumstances where the demands of justice require, a judge should discourage a party from requiring the judge to testify as a character witness.

Canon 2C. Florida Canon 2C is derived from a

recommendation by the American Bar Association and from the United States Senate Committee Resolution, 101st Congress, Second Session, as adopted by the United States Senate Judiciary Committee on August 2, 1990.

Membership of a judge in an organization that practices invidious discrimination gives rise to perceptions that the judge's impartiality is impaired. Whether an organization practices invidious discrimination is often a complex question to which judges should be sensitive. The answer cannot be determined from a mere examination of an organization's current membership rolls but rather depends on the history of the organization's selection of members and other relevant factors, such as that the organization is dedicated to the preservation of religious, ethnic, or cultural values of legitimate common interest to its members, or that it is in fact and effect an intimate, purely private organization whose membership limitations could not be constitutionally prohibited. See *New York State Club Ass'n Inc. v. City of New York*, 487 U.S. 1, 108 S.Ct. 2225, 101 L.Ed.2d 1 (1988); *Board of Directors of Rotary International v. Rotary Club of Duarte*, 481 U.S. 537, 107 S.Ct. 1940, 95 L.Ed.2d 474 (1987); *Roberts v. United States Jaycees*, 468 U.S. 609, 104 S.Ct. 3244, 82 L.Ed.2d 462 (1984). Other relevant factors include the size and nature of the organization and the diversity of persons in the locale who might reasonably be considered potential members. Thus the mere absence of diverse membership does not by itself demonstrate a violation unless reasonable persons with knowledge of all the relevant circumstances would expect that the membership would be diverse in the absence of invidious discrimination. Absent such factors, an organization is generally said to discriminate invidiously if it arbitrarily excludes from membership on the basis of race, religion, sex, or national origin persons who would otherwise be admitted to membership.

Canon 3

A Judge Shall Perform the Duties of Judicial Office Impartially and Diligently

This Canon is not intended to prohibit membership in religious and ethnic clubs, such as Knights of Columbus, Masons, B'nai B'rith, and Sons of Italy; civic organizations, such as Rotary, Kiwanis, and The Junior League; young people's organizations, such as Boy Scouts, Girl Scouts, Boy's Clubs, and Girl's Clubs; and charitable organizations, such as United Way and Red Cross.

Although Section 2C relates only to membership in

organizations that invidiously discriminate on the basis of race, sex, religion or national origin, a judge's membership in an organization that engages in any discriminatory membership practices prohibited by the law of the jurisdiction also violates Canon 2 and Section 2A and gives the appearance of impropriety. In addition, it would be a violation of Canon 2 and Section 2A for a judge to arrange a meeting at a club that the judge knows practices invidious discrimination on the basis of race, sex, religion or national origin in its membership or other policies, or for the judge to regularly use such a club. Moreover, public manifestation by a judge of the judge's knowing approval of invidious discrimination on any basis gives the appearance of impropriety under Canon 2 and diminishes public confidence in the integrity and impartiality of the judiciary, in violation of Section 2A.

When a person who is a judge on the date this Code becomes effective learns that an organization to which the judge belongs engages in invidious discrimination that would preclude membership under Section 2C or under Canon 2 and Section 2A, the judge is permitted, in lieu of resigning, to make immediate efforts to have the organization discontinue its invidiously discriminatory practices, but is required to suspend participation in any other activities of the organization.

If the organization fails to discontinue its invidiously discriminatory practices as promptly as possible (and in all events within a year of the judge's first learning of the practices), the judge is required to resign immediately from the organization

A. Judicial Duties in General.

The judicial duties of a judge take precedence over all the judge's other activities. The judge's judicial duties include all the duties of the judge's office prescribed by law. In the performance of these duties, the specific standards set forth in the following sections apply.

B. Adjudicative Responsibilities.

(1) A judge shall hear and decide matters assigned to the judge except those in which disqualification is required.

(2) A judge shall be faithful to the law and maintain professional competence in it. A judge shall not be swayed by partisan interests, public clamor, or fear of criticism.

(3) A judge shall require order and decorum in proceedings before the judge.

(4) A judge shall be patient, dignified, and courteous to litigants, jurors, witnesses, lawyers, and others with whom the judge deals in an official capacity, and shall

require similar conduct of lawyers, and of staff, court officials, and others subject to the judge's direction and control.

(5) A judge shall perform judicial duties without bias or prejudice. A judge shall not, in the performance of judicial duties, by words or conduct manifest bias or prejudice, including but not limited to bias or prejudice based upon race, sex, religion, national origin, disability, age, sexual orientation, or socioeconomic status, and shall not permit staff, court officials, and others subject to the judge's direction and control to do so. This section does not preclude the consideration of race, sex, religion, national origin, disability, age, sexual orientation, socioeconomic status, or other similar factors when they are issues in the proceeding.

(6) A judge shall require lawyers in proceedings before the judge to refrain from manifesting, by words, gestures, or other conduct, bias or prejudice based upon race, sex, religion, national origin, disability, age, sexual orientation, or socioeconomic status, against parties, witnesses, counsel, or others. This Section 3B(6) does not preclude legitimate advocacy when race, sex, religion, national origin, disability, age, sexual orientation, socioeconomic status, or other similar factors are issues in the proceeding.

(7) A judge shall accord to every person who has a legal interest in a proceeding, or that person's lawyer, the right to be heard according to law. A judge shall not initiate, permit, or consider ex parte communications, or consider other communications made to the judge outside the presence of the parties concerning a pending or impending proceeding except that:

(a) Where circumstances require, ex parte communications for scheduling, administrative purposes, or emergencies that do not deal with substantive matters or issues on the merits are authorized, provided:

(i) the judge reasonably believes that no party will gain a procedural or tactical advantage as a result of the ex parte communication, and

(ii) the judge makes provision promptly to notify all other parties of the substance of the ex parte communication and allows an opportunity to respond.

(b) A judge may obtain the advice of a disinterested expert on the law applicable to a proceeding before the judge if the judge gives notice to the parties of the person consulted and the substance of the advice and affords the parties reasonable opportunity to respond.

(c) A judge may consult with other judges or with court personnel whose function is to aid the judge in carrying out the judge's adjudicative responsibilities.

(d) A judge may, with the consent of the parties, confer separately with the parties and their lawyers in an effort to mediate or settle matters pending before the judge.

(e) A judge may initiate or consider any ex parte communications when expressly authorized by law to do so.

(8) A judge shall dispose of all judicial matters promptly, efficiently, and fairly.

(9) A judge shall not, while a proceeding is pending or impending in any court, make any public comment that might reasonably be expected to affect its outcome or impair its fairness or make any nonpublic comment that might substantially interfere with a fair trial or hearing. The judge shall require similar abstention on the part of court personnel subject to the judge's direction and control. This Section does not prohibit judges from making public statements in the course of their official duties or from explaining for public information the procedures of the court. This Section does not apply to proceedings in which the judge is a litigant in a personal capacity.

(10) A judge shall not, with respect to parties or classes of parties, cases, controversies or issues likely to come

before the court, make pledges, promises or commitments that are inconsistent with the impartial performance of the adjudicative duties of the office.

(11) A judge shall not commend or criticize jurors for their verdict other than in a court order or opinion in a proceeding, but may express appreciation to jurors for their service to the judicial system and the community.

(12) A judge shall not disclose or use, for any purpose unrelated to judicial duties, nonpublic information acquired in a judicial capacity.

C. Administrative Responsibilities.

(1) A judge shall diligently discharge the judge's administrative responsibilities without bias or prejudice and maintain professional competence in judicial administration, and should cooperate with other judges and court officials in the administration of court business.

(2) A judge shall require staff, court officials, and others subject to the judge's direction and control to observe the standards of fidelity and diligence that apply to the judge and to refrain from manifesting bias or prejudice in the performance of their official duties.

(3) A judge with supervisory authority for the judicial performance of other judges shall take reasonable measures to assure the prompt disposition of matters

before them and the proper performance of their other judicial responsibilities.

(4) A judge shall not make unnecessary appointments. A judge shall exercise the power of appointment impartially and on the basis of merit. A judge shall avoid nepotism and favoritism. A judge shall not approve compensation of appointees beyond the fair value of services rendered.

D. Disciplinary Responsibilities.

(1) A judge who receives information or has actual knowledge that substantial likelihood exists that another judge has committed a violation of this Code shall take appropriate action.

(2) A judge who receives information or has actual knowledge that substantial likelihood exists that a lawyer has committed a violation of the Rules Regulating The Florida Bar shall take appropriate action.

(3) Acts of a judge, in the discharge of disciplinary responsibilities, required or permitted by Sections 3D(1) and 3D(2) are part of a judge's judicial duties and shall be absolutely privileged, and no civil action predicated thereon may be instituted against the judge.

E. Disqualification.

(1) A judge shall disqualify himself or herself in a

proceeding in which the judge's impartiality might reasonably be questioned, including but not limited to instances where:

(a) the judge has a personal bias or prejudice concerning a party or a party's lawyer, or personal knowledge of disputed evidentiary facts concerning the proceeding;

(b) the judge served as a lawyer or was the lower court judge in the matter in controversy, or a lawyer with whom the judge previously practiced law served during such association as a lawyer concerning the matter, or the judge has been a material witness concerning it;

(c) the judge knows that he or she individually or as a fiduciary, or the judge's spouse, parent, or child wherever residing, or any other member of the judge's family residing in the judge's household has an economic interest in the subject matter in controversy or in a party to the proceeding or has any other more than de minimis interest that could be substantially affected by the proceeding;

(d) the judge or the judge's spouse, or a person within the third degree of relationship to either of them, or the spouse of such a person:

(i) is a party to the proceeding, or an officer, director, or trustee of a party;

(ii) is acting as a lawyer in the proceeding;

(iii) is known by the judge to have a more than de minimis interest that could be substantially affected by the proceeding;

(iv) is to the judge's knowledge likely to be a material witness in the proceeding;

(e) the judge's spouse or a person within the third degree of relationship to the judge participated as a lower court judge in a decision to be reviewed by the judge.

(f) the judge, while a judge or a candidate for judicial office, has made a public statement that commits, or appears to commit, the judge with respect to:

(i) parties or classes of parties in the proceeding;

(ii) an issue in the proceeding; or

(iii) the controversy in the proceeding.

(2) A judge should keep informed about the judge's personal and fiduciary economic interests, and make a reasonable effort to keep informed about the economic interests of the judge's spouse and minor children residing in the judge's household.

F. Remittal of Disqualification.

A judge disqualified by the terms of Section 3E may

disclose on the record the basis of the judge's disqualification and may ask the parties and their lawyers to consider, out of the presence of the judge, whether to waive disqualification. If following disclosure of any basis for disqualification other than personal bias or prejudice concerning a party, the parties and lawyers, without participation by the judge, all agree the judge should not be disqualified, and the judge is then willing to participate, the judge may participate in the proceeding. The agreement shall be incorporated in the record of the proceeding.

COMMENTARY

Canon 3B(4). The duty to hear all proceedings fairly and with patience is not inconsistent with the duty to dispose promptly of the business of the court. Judges can be efficient and business-like while being patient and deliberate.

Canon 3B(5). A judge must refrain from speech, gestures or other conduct that could reasonably be perceived as sexual harassment and must require the same standard of conduct of others subject to the judge's direction and control. A judge must perform judicial duties impartially and fairly. A judge who manifests bias on any basis in a proceeding impairs the fairness of the proceeding and brings the judiciary into disrepute. Facial expression and body language, in addition to oral communication, can give to parties or lawyers in the proceeding, jurors, the media and others an appearance of judicial bias. A judge must be alert to avoid behavior that may be perceived as prejudicial.

Canon 3B(7). The proscription against communications concerning a proceeding includes communications from lawyers, law teachers, and other persons who are not participants in the proceeding, except to the limited extent permitted.

To the extent reasonably possible, all parties or their lawyers shall be included in communications with a judge.

Whenever presence of a party or notice to a party is required by Section 3B(7), it is the party's lawyer, or if the party is unrepresented, the party who is to be present or to whom notice is to be given.

An appropriate and often desirable procedure for a court to obtain the advice of a disinterested expert on legal issues is to invite the expert to file a brief as amicus curiae.

Certain ex parte communication is approved by Section 3B(7) to facilitate scheduling and other administrative purposes and to accommodate emergencies. In general, however, a judge must discourage ex parte communication and allow it only if all the criteria stated in Section 3B(7) are clearly met. A judge must disclose to all parties all ex parte communications described in Sections 3B(7)(a) and 3B(7)(b) regarding a proceeding pending or impending before the judge. A judge must not independently investigate facts in a case and must consider only the evidence presented.

A judge may request a party to submit proposed findings of fact and conclusions of law, so long as the other parties are apprised of the request and are given an opportunity to respond to the proposed findings and conclusions.

A judge must make reasonable efforts, including the provision of appropriate supervision, to ensure that Section 3B(7) is not violated through law clerks or other personnel on the judge's staff.

If communication between the trial judge and the appellate court with respect to a proceeding is permitted, a copy of any written communication or the substance of any oral communication should be provided to all parties.

Canon 3B(8). In disposing of matters promptly, efficiently, and fairly, a judge must demonstrate due regard for the rights of the parties to be heard and to have issues resolved without unnecessary cost or delay.

Containing costs while preserving fundamental rights of parties also protects the interests of witnesses and the general public. A judge should monitor and supervise cases so as to reduce or eliminate dilatory practices, avoidable delays, and unnecessary costs. A judge should encourage and seek to facilitate settlement, but parties should not feel coerced into surrendering the right to have their controversy resolved by the courts.

Prompt disposition of the court's business requires a judge to devote adequate time to judicial duties, to be punctual in attending court and expeditious in determining matters under submission, and to insist that court officials, litigants, and their lawyers cooperate with the judge to that end.

Canon 3B(9) and 3B(10). Sections 3B(9) and (10) restrictions on judicial speech are essential to the maintenance of the integrity, impartiality, and independence of the judiciary. A pending proceeding is one that has begun but not yet reached final disposition. An impending proceeding is one that is anticipated but not yet begun. The requirement that judges abstain from public comment regarding a pending or impending proceeding continues during any appellate process and until final disposition. Sections 3B(9) and (10) do not prohibit a judge from commenting on proceedings in which the judge is a litigant in a personal capacity, but in cases such as a writ of mandamus where the judge is a litigant in an official capacity, the judge must not comment publicly. The conduct of lawyers relating to trial publicity is governed by Rule 4-3.6 of the Rules Regulating The Florida Bar.

Canon 3B(10). Commending or criticizing jurors for their verdict may imply a judicial expectation in future cases and may impair a juror's ability to be fair and impartial in a subsequent case.

Canon 3C(4). Appointees of a judge include assigned counsel, officials such as referees, commissioners, special magistrates, receivers, mediators, arbitrators, and guardians and personnel such as clerks, secretaries, and bailiffs. Consent by the parties to an appointment or an award of compensation does not relieve the judge of the obligation prescribed by Section 3C(4). See also Fla.Stat. § 112.3135 (1991).

Canon 3D. Appropriate action may include direct communication with the judge or lawyer who has committed the violation, other direct action if available, or reporting the violation to the appropriate authority or other agency. If the conduct is minor, the Canon allows a judge to address the problem solely by direct communication with the offender. A judge having knowledge, however, that another judge has committed a violation of this Code that raises a substantial question as to that other judge's fitness for office or has knowledge that a lawyer has committed a violation of the Rules of Professional Conduct that raises a substantial question as to the lawyer's honesty, trustworthiness or fitness as a lawyer in other respects, is required under this Canon to inform the appropriate authority. While worded differently, this Code provision has the identical purpose as the related Model Code provisions.

Canon 3E(1). Under this rule, a judge is disqualified whenever the judge's impartiality might reasonably be questioned, regardless of whether any of the specific rules in Section 3E(1) apply. For example, if a judge were in the process of negotiating for employment with a law firm, the judge would be disqualified from any matters in which that law firm appeared, unless the disqualification was waived by the parties after disclosure by the judge.

A judge should disclose on the record information that the judge believes the parties or their lawyers might consider relevant to the question of disqualification, even if the judge believes there is no real basis for disqualification. The fact that the judge conveys this information does not automatically require the judge to be disqualified upon a request by either party, but the issue should be resolved on a case-by-case basis. Similarly, if a lawyer or party has previously filed a complaint against the judge with the Judicial Qualifications Commission, that the fact does not automatically require disqualification of the judge. Such disqualification should be on a case-by-case basis.

By decisional law, the rule of necessity may override the rule of disqualification. For example, a judge might be required to participate in judicial review of a judicial salary statute, or might be the only judge available in a matter requiring immediate judicial action, such as a hearing on probable cause or a temporary restraining order. In the latter case, the judge must disclose on the record the basis for possible disqualification and use reasonable efforts to transfer the matter to another judge as soon as practicable.

Canon 3E(1)(b). A lawyer in a government agency does not ordinarily have an association with other lawyers employed by that agency within the meaning of Section 3E(1)(b); a judge formerly employed by a government agency, however, should disqualify himself or herself in a proceeding if the judge's impartiality might reasonably be questioned because of such association.

Canon 3E(1)(d). The fact that a lawyer in a proceeding is affiliated with a law firm with which a relative of the judge is affiliated does not of itself disqualify the judge. Under appropriate circumstances, the fact that "the judge's impartiality might reasonably be questioned" under Section 3E(1), or that the relative is known by the judge to have an interest in the law firm that could be "substantially affected by the outcome of the proceeding" under Section 3E(1)(d)(iii) may require the judge's disqualification.

Canon 3E(1)(e). It is not uncommon for a judge's spouse or a person within the third degree of relationship to a judge to also serve as a judge in either the trial or appellate courts. However, where a judge exercises appellate authority over another judge, and that other judge is either a spouse or a relationship within the third degree, then this Code requires disqualification of the judge that is exercising appellate authority. This Code, under these circumstances, precludes the appellate judge from participating in the review of the spouse's or relation's case.

Canon 3F. A remittal procedure provides the parties an opportunity to proceed without delay if they wish to waive the disqualification. To assure that consideration of the question of remittal is made independently of the judge, a judge must not solicit, seek, or hear comment on possible remittal or waiver of the disqualification unless the lawyers jointly propose remittal after consultation as provided in the rule. A party may act through counsel if counsel represents on the record that the party has been consulted and consents. As a practical matter, a judge may wish to have all parties and their lawyers sign the remittal agreement.

Canon 4

A Judge Is Encouraged to Engage in Activities to Improve the Law, the Legal System, and the Administration of Justice

A. A judge shall conduct all of the judge's quasi-judicial activities so that they do not:
(1) cast reasonable doubt on the judge's capacity to act impartially as a judge;
(2) undermine the judge's independence, integrity, or impartiality;
(3) demean the judicial office;
(4) interfere with the proper performance of judicial duties;
(5) lead to frequent disqualification of the judge; or
(6) appear to a reasonable person to be coercive.
B. A judge is encouraged to speak, write, lecture, teach and participate in other quasi-judicial activities concerning the law, the legal system, the administration

of justice, and the role of the judiciary as an independent branch within our system of government, subject to the requirements of this Code.

C. A judge shall not appear at a public hearing before, or otherwise consult with, an executive or legislative body or official except on matters concerning the law, the legal system or the administration of justice or except when acting pro se in a matter involving the judge or the judge's interests.

D. A judge is encouraged to serve as a member, officer, director, trustee or non-legal advisor of an organization or governmental entity devoted to the improvement of the law, the legal system, the judicial branch, or the administration of justice, subject to the following limitations and the other requirements of this Code.

(1) A judge shall not serve as an officer, director, trustee or non-legal advisor if it is likely that the organization

(a) will be engaged in proceedings that would ordinarily come before the judge, or

(b) will be engaged frequently in adversary proceedings in the court of which the judge is a member or in any court subject to the appellate jurisdiction of the court of which the judge is a member.

(2) A judge as an officer, director, trustee or non-legal

advisor, or as a member or otherwise:

(a) may assist such an organization in planning fund-raising and may participate in the management and investment of the organization's funds, but shall not personally or directly participate in the solicitation of funds, except that a judge may solicit funds from other judges over whom the judge does not exercise supervisory or appellate authority;

(b) may appear or speak at, receive an award or other recognition at, be featured on the program of, and permit the judge's title to be used in conjunction with an event of such an organization or entity, but if the event serves a fund-raising purpose, the judge may participate only if the event concerns the law, the legal system, or the administration of justice and the funds raised will be used for a law related purpose(s);

(c) may make recommendations to public and private fund-granting organizations on projects and programs concerning the law, the legal system or the administration of justice;

(d) shall not personally or directly participate in membership solicitation if the solicitation might reasonably be perceived as coercive;

(e) shall not make use of court premises, staff, stationery, equipment, or other resources for fund-raising purposes, except for incidental use for activities that concern the law, the legal system, or the administration of justice, subject to the requirements of this Code.

COMMENTARY

Canon 4A. A judge is encouraged to participate in activities designed to improve the law, the legal system, and the administration of justice. In doing so, however, it must be understood that expressions of bias or prejudice by a judge, even outside the judge's judicial activities, may cast reasonable doubt on the judge's capacity to act impartially as a judge and may undermine the independence and integrity of the judiciary. Expressions which may do so include jokes or other remarks demeaning individuals on the basis of their race, sex, religion, national origin, disability, age, sexual orientation or socioeconomic status. See Canon 2C and accompanying Commentary.

Canon 4B. This canon was clarified in order to encourage judges to engage in activities to improve the law, the legal system, and the administration of justice. As a judicial officer and person specially learned in the law, a judge is in a unique position to contribute to the improvement of the law, the legal system, and the administration of justice, including, but not limited to, the improvement of the role of the judiciary as an independent branch of government, the revision of substantive and procedural law, the improvement of criminal and juvenile justice, and the improvement of justice in the areas of civil, criminal, family, domestic violence, juvenile delinquency, juvenile dependency, probate and motor vehicle law. To the extent that time permits, a judge is encouraged to do so, either independently or through a bar association, judicial conference or other organization dedicated to the improvement of the law. Support of pro bono legal services by members of the bench is an activity that relates to improvement of the administration of justice. Accordingly, a judge may engage in activities intended to encourage attorneys to perform pro bono services, including, but not limited to: participating in events to recognize attorneys who do pro bono work, establishing general procedural or scheduling accommodations for pro bono attorneys as feasible, and acting in an advisory capacity to pro bono programs. Judges are encouraged to participate in efforts to promote the fair administration of justice, the independence of the judiciary and the integrity of the legal profession, which may include the expression of opposition to the persecution of lawyers and judges in other countries.

The phrase "subject to the requirements of this Code" is

included to remind judges that the use of permissive language in various sections of the Code does not relieve a judge from the other requirements of the Code that apply to the specific conduct.

Canon 4C. See Canon 2B regarding the obligation to avoid improper influence.

Canon 4D(1). The changing nature of some organizations and of their relationship to the law makes it necessary for a judge regularly to reexamine the activities of each organization with which the judge is affiliated to determine if it is proper for the judge to continue the affiliation. For example, the boards of some legal aid organizations now make policy decisions that may have political significance or imply commitment to causes that may come before the courts for adjudication.

Canon 4D(2). A judge may solicit membership or endorse or encourage membership efforts for an organization devoted to the improvement of the law, the legal system or the administration of justice as long as the solicitation cannot reasonably be perceived as coercive. Personal or direct solicitation of funds for an organization and personal or direct solicitation of memberships involve the danger that the person solicited will feel obligated to respond favorably to the solicitor if the solicitor is in a position of influence or control. A judge must not engage in direct, individual solicitation of funds or memberships in person, in writing or by telephone except in the following cases: 1) a judge may solicit for funds or memberships other judges over whom the judge does not exercise supervisory or appellate authority, 2) a judge may solicit other persons for membership in the organizations described above if neither those persons nor persons with whom they are affiliated are likely ever to appear before the court on which the judge serves and 3) a judge who is an officer of such an organization may send a general membership solicitation mailing over the judge's signature.

A judge may be a speaker or guest of honor at an organization's fund-raising event if the event concerns the law, the legal system, or the administration of justice, and the judge does not engage in the direct solicitation of funds. However, judges may not participate in or allow their titles to be used in connection with fund-raising activities on behalf of an organization engaging in advocacy if such participation would cast doubt on the judge's capacity to act impartially as a judge.

Use of an organization letterhead for fund-raising or membership solicitation does not violate Canon 4D(2) provided the letterhead lists only the judge's name and office or other position in the organization, and, if comparable designations are listed for other persons, the judge's judicial designation. In addition, a judge must also make reasonable efforts to ensure that the judge's staff, court officials and others subject to the judge's direction and control do not solicit funds on the judge's behalf for any purpose, charitable or otherwise.

Canon 5

A Judge Shall Regulate Extrajudicial Activities to Minimize the Risk of Conflict with Judicial Duties

A JUDGE SHALL REGULATE EXTRAJUDICIAL ACTIVITIES TO MINIMIZE THE RISK OF CONFLICT WITH JUDICIAL DUTIES
A. Extrajudicial Activities in General. A judge shall conduct all of the judge's extra-judicial activities so that they do not:
(1) cast reasonable doubt on the judge's capacity to act impartially as a judge;
(2) undermine the judge's independence, integrity, or impartiality;
(3) demean the judicial office;
(4) interfere with the proper performance of judicial duties;
(5) lead to frequent disqualification of the judge; or

(6) appear to a reasonable person to be coercive.

B. Avocational Activities. A judge is encouraged to speak, write, lecture, teach and participate in other extrajudicial activities concerning non-legal subjects, subject to the requirements of this Code.

C. Governmental, Civic or Charitable Activities.

(1) A judge shall not appear at a public hearing before, or otherwise consult with, an executive or legislative body or official except on matters concerning the law, the legal system or the administration of justice or except when acting pro se in a matter involving the judge or the judge's interests.

(2) A judge shall not accept appointment to a governmental committee or commission or other governmental position that is concerned with issues of fact or policy on matters other than the improvement of the law, the legal system, the judicial branch, or the administration of justice. A judge may, however, represent a country, state or locality on ceremonial occasions or in connection with historical, educational or cultural activities.

(3) A judge may serve as an officer, director, trustee or non-legal advisor of an educational, religious, charitable, fraternal, sororal or civic organization not conducted for profit, subject to the following limitations and the other requirements of this Code.

(a) A judge shall not serve as an officer, director, trustee or non-legal advisor if it is likely that the organization
(i) will be engaged in proceedings that would ordinarily come before the judge, or
(ii) will be engaged frequently in adversary proceedings in the court of which the judge is a member or in any court subject to the appellate jurisdiction of the court of which the judge is a member.
(b) A judge as an officer, director, trustee or non-legal advisor, or as a member or otherwise:
(i) may assist such an organization in planning fund-raising and may participate in the management and investment of the organization's funds, but shall not personally or directly participate in the solicitation of funds, except that a judge may solicit funds from other judges over whom the judge does not exercise supervisory or appellate authority;
(ii) shall not personally or directly participate in membership solicitation if the solicitation might reasonably be perceived as coercive;
(iii) shall not use or permit the use of the prestige of judicial office for fund-raising or membership solicitation.
D. Financial Activities.
(1) A judge shall not engage in financial and business dealings that
(a) may reasonably be perceived to exploit the judge's

judicial position, or
(b) involve the judge in frequent transactions or continuing business relationships with those lawyers or other persons likely to come before the court on which the judge serves.

(2) A judge may, subject to the requirements of this Code, hold and manage investments of the judge and members of the judge's family, including real estate, and engage in other remunerative activity.

(3) A judge shall not serve as an officer, director, manager, general partner, advisor or employee of any business entity except that a judge may, subject to the requirements of this Code, manage and participate in:
(a) a business closely held by the judge or members of the judge's family, or
(b) a business entity primarily engaged in investment of the financial resources of the judge or members of the judge's family.

(4) A judge shall manage the judge's investments and other financial interests to minimize the number of cases in which the judge is disqualified. As soon as the judge can do so without serious financial detriment, the judge shall divest himself or herself of investments and other financial interests that might require frequent disqualification.

(5) A judge shall not accept, and shall urge members of

the judge's family residing in the judge's household not to accept, a gift, bequest, favor or loan from anyone except for:

(a) a gift incident to a public testimonial, books, tapes and other resource materials supplied by publishers on a complimentary basis for official use, or an invitation to the judge and the judge's spouse or guest to attend a bar-related function or an activity devoted to the improvement of the law, the legal system or the administration of justice, including attending, without charge, a bar-related lunch, dinner, or social event; and if the value of attending an individual function or event exceeds $100, the judge shall report it under Canon 6B(2);

(b) a gift, award or benefit incident to the business, profession or other separate activity of a spouse or other family member of a judge residing in the judge's household, including gifts, awards and benefits for the use of both the spouse or other family member and the judge (as spouse or family member), provided the gift, award or benefit could not reasonably be perceived as intended to influence the judge in the performance of judicial duties;

(c) ordinary social hospitality;

(d) a gift from a relative or friend, for a special occasion, such as a wedding, anniversary or birthday, if the gift is fairly commensurate with the occasion and the relationship;

(e) a gift, bequest, favor or loan from a relative or close personal friend whose appearance or interest in a case would in any event require disqualification under Canon 3E;

(f) a loan from a lending institution in its regular course of business on the same terms generally available to persons who are not judges;

(g) a scholarship or fellowship awarded on the same terms and based on the same criteria applied to other applicants; or

(h) any other gift, bequest, favor or loan, only if the donor is not a party or other person who has come or is likely to come or whose interests have come or are likely to come before the judge; and, if its value, or the aggregate value in a calendar year of such gifts, bequests, favors, or loans from a single source, exceeds $100.00, the judge reports it in the same manner as the judge reports gifts under Canon 6B(2)

E. Fiduciary Activities.

(1) A judge shall not serve as executor, administrator or other personal representative, trustee, guardian, attorney in fact or other fiduciary, except for the estate, trust or person of a member of the judge's family, and then only if such service will not interfere with the proper

performance of judicial duties.

(2) A judge shall not serve as a fiduciary if it is likely that the judge as a fiduciary will be engaged in proceedings that would ordinarily come before the judge, or if the estate, trust or ward becomes involved in adversary proceedings in the court on which the judge serves or one under its appellate jurisdiction.

(3) The same restrictions on financial activities that apply to a judge personally also apply to the judge while acting in a fiduciary capacity.

F. Service as Arbitrator or Mediator.

(1) A judge shall not act as an arbitrator or mediator or otherwise perform judicial functions in a private capacity unless expressly authorized by law or Court rule. A judge may, however, take the necessary educational and training courses required to be a qualified and certified arbitrator or mediator, and may fulfill the requirements of observing and conducting actual arbitration or mediation proceedings as part of the certification process, provided such program does not, in any way, interfere with the performance of the judge's judicial duties.

(2) A senior judge may serve as a mediator in a case in a circuit in which the senior judge is presiding over criminal cases or in a circuit in which the senior judge is not presiding as a judge, or in both, only if the senior judge is certified pursuant to rule 10.100, Florida Rules

for Certified and Court-Appointed Mediators. Such senior judge may be associated with entities that are solely engaged in offering mediation or other alternative dispute resolution services but that are not otherwise engaged in the practice of law. However, such senior judge may not advertise, solicit business, associate with a law firm, or participate in any other activity that directly or indirectly promotes his or her mediation, arbitration, or voluntary trial resolution services and shall not permit an entity with which the senior judge associates to do so. A senior judge shall not serve as a mediator, arbitrator, or voluntary trial resolution judge in any case in a circuit in which the judge is currently presiding over civil cases as a senior judge. A senior judge who provides mediation, arbitration, or voluntary trial resolution services may preside over criminal cases in circuits in which the judge provides such dispute-resolution services. A senior judge who provides mediation, arbitration, or voluntary trial resolution services may also preside over civil and criminal cases in circuits in which the judge does not provide such dispute-resolution services. A senior judge shall disclose if the judge is being utilized or has been utilized as a mediator, arbitrator, or voluntary trial resolution judge by any party, attorney, or law firm involved in the case pending before the senior judge. Absent express consent of all parties, a senior judge is prohibited from presiding over any case involving any party, attorney, or law firm that is utilizing or has utilized the judge as a mediator, arbitrator, or voluntary trial resolution judge within the previous three years. A senior judge shall disclose any negotiations or agreements for the provision of services as a mediator, arbitrator, or voluntary trial resolution judge between the senior judge and any parties or counsel to the case.

G. Practice of Law. A judge shall not practice law. Notwithstanding this prohibition, a judge may act pro se and may, without compensation, give legal advice to and draft or review documents for a member of the judge's family.

[Amended Jan. 10, 2002 (816 So. 2d 1084); Feb. 20, 2003 (840 So. 2d 1023); Nov. 3, 2005, effective Jan. 1, 2006 (915 So. 2d 145); 983 So. 2d 550); June 19, 2014 (141 So. 3d 1172); July 7, 2016, effective Oct. 1, 2016 (194 So. 3d 1015); May 18, 2017, effective Jan. 1, 2017 (218 So. 3d 432); In re Amendments to the Code of Judicial Conduct, No. SC21-737 (Fla. May 21, 2021).]

Canon 5A. Complete separation of a judge from extra-judicial activities is neither possible nor wise; a judge should not become isolated from the community in which the judge lives. For that reason, judges are encouraged to participate in extrajudicial community activities.

Expressions of bias or prejudice by a judge, even outside the judge's judicial activities, may cast reasonable doubt on the judge's capacity to act impartially as a judge and may undermine the independence and integrity of the judiciary. Expressions which may do so include jokes or other remarks demeaning individuals on the basis of their race, sex, religion, national origin, disability, age, sexual orientation or socioeconomic status. See Canon 2C and accompanying Commentary.

Canon 5B. In this and other sections of Canon 5, the phrase "subject to the requirements of this Code" is used, notably in connection with a judge's governmental, civic or charitable activities. This phrase is included to remind judges that the use of permissive language in various sections of the Code does not relieve a judge from the other requirements of the Code that apply to the specific conduct. Canon 5C(1). See Canon 2B regarding the obligation to avoid improper influence.

Canon 5C(2). Canon 5C(2) prohibits a judge from accepting any governmental position except one relating to the law, legal system or administration of justice as authorized by Canon 4D. The appropriateness of accepting extrajudicial assignments must be assessed in light of the demands on judicial resources created by crowded dockets and the need to protect the courts from involvement in extrajudicial matters that may prove to be controversial. Judges should not accept governmental appointments that are likely to interfere with the effectiveness and independence of the judiciary.

Canon 5C(2) does not govern a judge's service in a nongovernmental position. See Canon 5C(3) permitting service by a judge with educational, religious, charitable, fraternal, sororal or civic organizations not conducted for profit. For example, service on the board of a public educational institution, unless it were a law school, would be prohibited under Canon 5C(2), but service on the board of a public law school or any private educational institution would generally be permitted under Canon 5C(3).

Canon 5C(3). Canon 5C(3) does not apply to a judge's service in a governmental position unconnected with the improvement of the law, the legal system or the administration of justice; see Canon 5C(2).

See Commentary to Canon 5B regarding use of the phrase "subject to the following limitations and the other requirements of this Code." As an example of the meaning of the phrase, a judge permitted by Canon 5C(3) to serve on the board of a fraternal institution may be prohibited from such service by Canons 2C or 5A if the institution practices invidious discrimination or if service on the board otherwise casts reasonable doubt on the judge's capacity to act impartially as a judge.

Service by a judge on behalf of a civic or charitable organization may be governed by other provisions of Canon 5 in addition to Canon 5C. For example, Canon 5G prohibits a judge from serving as a legal advisor to a civic or charitable organization.

Canon 5C(3)(a). The changing nature of some organizations and of their relationship to the law makes it necessary for a judge to regularly reexamine the activities of each organization with which the judge is affiliated in order to determine if it is proper for the judge to continue the affiliation. For example, in many jurisdictions charitable hospitals are now more frequently in court than in the past.

Canon 5C(3)(b). A judge may solicit membership or endorse or encourage membership efforts for a nonprofit educational, religious, charitable, fraternal, sororal or civic organization as long as the solicitation cannot reasonably be perceived as coercive and is not essentially a fund-raising mechanism. Personal or direct solicitation of funds for an organization and personal or direct solicitation of memberships similarly involve the danger that the person solicited will feel obligated to respond favorably to the solicitor if the solicitor is in a position of influence or control. A judge must not engage in direct, individual solicitation of funds or memberships in person, in writing or by telephone except in the following cases: 1) a judge may solicit for funds or memberships other judges over whom the judge does not exercise supervisory or appellate authority, 2) a judge may solicit other persons for membership in the organizations described above if neither those persons nor persons with whom they are affiliated are likely ever to appear before the court on which the judge serves and 3) a judge who is an officer of such an organization may send a general membership solicitation mailing over the judge's signature.

Mere attendance at an event, whether or not the event serves a fund-raising purpose, does not constitute a violation of Canon 5C(3)(b). It is also generally permissible for a judge to pass a collection plate at a place of worship or for a judge to serve as an usher or food server or preparer, or to perform similar subsidiary and unadvertised functions at fund-raising events sponsored by educational, religious, charitable, fraternal, or civic organizations, so long as they do not entail direct or personal solicitation. However, a judge may not be a speaker, guest of honor, or otherwise be featured at an organization's fund-raising event, unless the event concerns the law, the legal system, or the administration of justice as authorized by Canon 4D(2)(b). Use of an organization letterhead for fund-raising or membership solicitation does not violate Canon 5C(3)(b) provided the letterhead lists only the judge's name and office or other position in the organization, and, if comparable designations are listed for other persons, the judge's judicial designation. In addition, a judge must also make reasonable efforts to ensure that the judge's staff, court officials and others subject to the judge's direction and control do not solicit funds on the judge's behalf for any purpose, charitable or otherwise.

Canon 5D(1). When a judge acquires in a judicial capacity information, such as material contained in filings with the court, that is not yet generally known, the judge must not use the information for private gain. See Canon 2B; see also Canon 3B(11).

A judge must avoid financial and business dealings that involve the judge in frequent transactions or continuing business relationships with persons likely to come either before the judge personally or before other judges on the judge's court. In addition, a judge should discourage members of the judge's family from engaging in dealings that would reasonably appear to exploit the judge's judicial position. This rule is necessary to avoid creating an appearance of exploitation of office or favoritism and to minimize the potential for disqualification. With respect to affiliation of relatives of the judge with law firms appearing before the judge, see Commentary to Canon 3E(1) relating to disqualification.

Participation by a judge in financial and business dealings is subject to the general prohibitions in Canon 5A against activities that tend to reflect adversely on impartiality, demean the judicial office, or interfere with the proper performance of judicial duties. Such participation is also subject to the general prohibition in Canon 2 against activities involving impropriety or the appearance of impropriety and the prohibition in Canon 2B against the misuse of the prestige of judicial office. In addition, a judge must maintain high standards of conduct in all of the judge's activities, as set forth in Canon 1. See Commentary for Canon 5B regarding use of the phrase "subject to the requirements of this Code." Canon 5D(2). This Canon provides that, subject to the requirements of this Code, a judge may hold and manage investments owned solely by the judge, investments owned solely by a member or members of the judge's family, and investments owned jointly by the judge and members of the judge's family. Canon 5D(3). Subject to the requirements of this Code, a judge may participate in a business that is closely held either by the judge alone, by members of the judge's family, or by the judge and members of the judge's family.

Although participation by a judge in a closely-held family business might otherwise be permitted by Canon 5D(3), a judge may be prohibited from participation by other provisions of this Code when, for example, the business entity frequently appears before the judge's court or the participation requires significant time away from judicial duties. Similarly, a judge must avoid participating in a closely-held family business if the judge's participation would involve misuse of the prestige of judicial office.

Canon 5D(5). Canon 5D(5) does not apply to contributions to a judge's campaign for judicial office, a matter governed by Canon 7 .

Because a gift, bequest, favor or loan to a member of the judge's family residing in the judge's household might be viewed as intended to influence the judge, a judge must inform those family members of the relevant ethical constraints upon the judge in this regard and discourage those family members from violating them.

A judge cannot, however, reasonably be expected to know or control all of the financial or business activities of all family members residing in the judge's household. Canon 5D(5)(a). Acceptance of an invitation to a law-related function is governed by Canon 5D(5)(a); acceptance of an invitation paid for by an individual lawyer or group of lawyers is governed by Canon

5D(5)(h).

The attendance, without charge, of a bar-related lunch, dinner, or social event such as a reception or Law Day event does not have to be reported under Canon 6B(2), as long as the actual value of attending the individual function or event does not exceed $100, despite the fact that the aggregate value of attending such functions or events given by the same bar association or other entity in the same calendar year exceeds $100. This differs from Rule 3.15 of the American Bar Association Model Code of Judicial Conduct (2011), which requires the reporting of such attendance if the value of attending such functions or events alone or in the aggregate from the same source in the same calendar year exceeds a specified amount.

A judge may accept a public testimonial or a gift incident thereto only if the donor organization is not an organization whose members comprise or frequently represent the same side in litigation, and the testimonial and gift are otherwise in compliance with other provisions of this Code. See Canons 5A(1) and 2B.

Canon 5D(5)(d). A gift to a judge, or to a member of the judge's family living in the judge's household, that is excessive in value raises questions about the judge's impartiality and the integrity of the judicial office and might require disqualification of the judge where disqualification would not otherwise be required. See, however, Canon 5D(5)(e).

Canon 5D(5)(h). Canon 5D(5)(h) prohibits judges from accepting gifts, favors, bequests or loans from lawyers or their firms if they have come or are likely to come before the judge; it also prohibits gifts, favors, bequests or loans from clients of lawyers or their firms when the clients' interests have come or are likely to come before the judge.

Canon 5E(3). The restrictions imposed by this Canon may conflict with the judge's obligation as a fiduciary. For example, a judge should resign as trustee if detriment to the trust would result from divestiture of holdings the retention of which would place the judge in violation of Canon 5D(4).

Canon 5F(1). Canon 5F(1) does not prohibit a judge from participating in arbitration, mediation or settlement conferences performed as part of judicial duties. An active judge may take the necessary educational and training programs to be certified or qualified as a mediator or arbitrator, but this shall not be a part of the judge's judicial duties. While such a course will allow a judge to have a better understanding of the arbitration and mediation process, the certification and qualification of a judge as a mediator or arbitrator is primarily for the judge's personal benefit. While actually participating in the mediation and arbitration training activities, care must be taken in the selection of both cases and locations so as to guarantee that there is no interference or conflict between the training and the judge's judicial responsibilities. Indeed, the training should be conducted in such a manner as to avoid the involvement of persons likely to appear before the judge in legal proceedings.

Canon 5F(2). The purpose of the admonitions in this canon is to ensure that the impartiality of a senior judge is not subject to question. Although a senior judge may act as a mediator, arbitrator, or voluntary trial resolution judge in a circuit in which the judge is presiding over criminal cases or in a circuit in which the judge is not presiding as a senior judge, or in both, attention must be given to relationships with lawyers and law firms which may require disclosure or disqualification. These provisions are intended to prohibit a senior judge from soliciting lawyers to use the senior judge's mediation services when those lawyers are or may be before the judge in proceedings where the senior judge is acting in a judicial capacity and to require a senior judge to ensure that entities with which the senior judge associates as a mediator abide by the same prohibitions on advertising or promoting the senior judge's mediation service as are imposed on the senior judge.

Canon 5G. This prohibition refers to the practice of law in a representative capacity and not in a pro se capacity. A judge may act for himself or herself in all legal matters, including matters involving litigation and matters involving appearances before or other dealings with legislative and other governmental bodies. However, in so doing, a judge must not abuse the prestige of office to advance the interests of the judge or the judge's family. See Canon 2B.

The Code allows a judge to give legal advice to and draft legal documents for members of the judge's family, so long as the judge receives no compensation. A judge must not, however, act as an advocate or negotiator for a member of the judge's family in a legal matter.

[Commentary amended Feb. 20, 2003 (840 So. 2d 1023); Nov. 3, 2005, effective Jan. 1, 2006 (915 So. 2d 145); May 22, 2008 (983 So. 2d 550); June 19, 2014 (141 So. 3d 1172); July 7, 2016, effective Oct. 1, 2016 (194 So. 3d 1015) ; May 18, 2017, effective Jan. 1, 2017 (So. 3d).]

Canon 6

Fiscal Matters of a Judge Shall Be Conducted in a Manner That Does Not Give the Appearance of

Influence or Impropriety

Fiscal Matters of a Judge Shall be Conducted in a Manner That Does Not Give the Appearance of Influence or Impropriety; a Judge Shall Regularly File Public Reports as Required by Article II, Section 8, of the Constitution of Florida, and Shall Publicly Report Gifts, Expense Reimbursements and Payments, and Waivers of Fees or Charges; Additional Financial Information Shall be Filed With the Judicial Qualifications Commission to Ensure Full Financial Disclosure

A. Compensation for Quasi-Judicial and Extrajudicial Services and Reimbursement or Payment of Expenses, and Waiver of Fees or Charges. A judge may accept compensation, reimbursement, or direct payment of expenses, and a waiver or partial waiver of fees or charges for registration, tuition, and similar items associated with the judge's participation in quasi-judicial and extrajudicial activities permitted by this Code, if the source of such payments, or waiver does not give the appearance of influencing the judge in the performance of judicial duties or otherwise give the appearance of impropriety, subject to the following restrictions: (1) Compensation. Compensation shall not exceed a reasonable amount nor shall it exceed what a person who is not a judge would receive for the same activity.

Compensation is reportable as income under Canon 6B(1). (2) Honoraria and Speaking Fees. A judge may accept honoraria and speaking fees that are reasonable and commensurate with the task performed. Honoraria and speaking fees are reportable as income under Canon 6B(1). (3) Reimbursement or Payment of Expenses, and Waiver of Fees or Charges. Expense reimbursement shall be limited to the actual cost of travel, food, and lodging reasonably incurred by the judge and, where appropriate to the occasion, to the judge's spouse. Any payment in excess of such an amount is compensation and is reportable as income under Canon 6B(1). Reimbursement or direct payment of expenses, and waiver or partial waiver of fees or charges for the judge or the judge's spouse or guest, from sources other than the state or a judicial branch entity as defined in Florida Rule of Judicial Administration 2.420(b)(2), the amount of which alone or in the aggregate with other reimbursements, payments, or waivers received from the same source in the same calendar year exceeds $100, shall be reported under Canon 6B(2). B. Public Financial Reporting. (1) Income and Assets. A judge shall file such public report as may be required by law for all public officials to comply fully with the provisions of Article II, Section 8, of the Constitution of Florida . The form for public financial disclosure shall be that recommended or adopted by the Florida Commission on Ethics for use by all public officials. The form shall be filed with the Florida Commission on Ethics on the date prescribed by law, and a copy shall be filed simultaneously with the Judicial Qualifications Commission. (2) Gifts, Reimbursements or Payments of Expenses, and Waivers of Fees or Charges. A judge shall file a public report of all gifts required to be disclosed under Canons 5D(5)(a) and 5D(5)(h) of the Code of Judicial Conduct, and of all reimbursements or direct payments of expenses, and waivers of fees or charges required to be disclosed under Canon 6A(3). The report of gifts, expense reimbursements or direct payments, and waivers received in the preceding calendar year shall be filed with the Florida Commission on Ethics on or before July 1 of each year. Disclosure shall be made using Form 6A in the commentary below. A copy shall be filed simultaneously with the Judicial Qualifications Commission. (3) Disclosure of Financial Interests Upon Leaving Office. A judge shall file a final disclosure statement within 60 days after leaving office, which report shall cover the period between January 1 of the year in which the judge leaves office and his or her last day of office, unless, within the 60-day period, the judge takes another public position requiring financial disclosure under Article II, Section 8, of the Constitution of Florida , or is otherwise required to file full and public disclosure for the final disclosure period. The form for disclosure of financial interests upon leaving office shall be that recommended or adopted by the Florida Commission on Ethics for use by all public officials. The form shall be filed with the Florida Commission on Ethics and a copy shall be filed simultaneously with the Judicial Qualifications Commission. C. Confidential Financial Reporting to the Judicial Qualifications Commission. To ensure that complete financial information is available for all judicial officers, there shall be filed with the Judicial Qualifications Commission on or before July 1 of each year, if not already included in the public report to be filed under Canon 6B(1) and (2), a verified list of the names of the corporations and other business entities in which the judge has a financial interest as of December 31 of the preceding year, which shall be transmitted in a separate sealed envelope, placed by the Commission in safekeeping, and not be opened or the contents thereof disclosed except in the manner hereinafter provided. At any time during or after the pendency of a cause, any party may request information as to whether the most recent list filed by the judge or judges before whom the cause is or was pending contains the name of any specific person or corporation or other business entity which is a party to the cause or which has a substantial direct or indirect financial interest in its outcome. Neither the making of the request nor the contents thereof shall be revealed by the chair to any judge or other person except at the instance of the individual making the request. If the request meets the requirements hereinabove set forth, the chair shall render a prompt answer thereto and thereupon return the report to safekeeping for retention in accordance with the provisions hereinabove stated. All such requests shall be verified and transmitted to the chair of the Commission on forms to be approved by it. D. Limitation of Disclosure. Disclosure of a judge's income, debts, investments or other assets is required only to the extent provided in this Canon and in Sections 3E and 3F, or as otherwise required by law. [Amended Jan. 10, 2002 (816 So. 2d 1084); May 18, 2017, effective Jan. 1, 2017 (218 So. 3d 432); May 10, 2018 (242 So. 3d 319).]

COMMENTARY

Canon 6A. See Section 5D(5)(a)–(h) regarding reporting of gifts, bequests and loans.

The Code does not prohibit a judge from accepting honoraria or speaking fees provided that the compensation is reasonable and commensurate with the task performed. A judge should ensure, however, that no conflicts are created by the arrangement. Judges must not appear to trade on the judicial position for personal advantage. Nor should a judge spend significant time away from court duties to meet speaking or writing commitments for compensation. In addition, the source of the payment must not raise any question of undue influence or the judge's ability or willingness to be impartial.

Canon 6A(3) requires a judge to report expense reimbursements or payments, and fee waivers from sources other than the state or a judicial branch entity, when the amount received alone or combined with other reimbursements, payments, or waivers received from the same source in the same calendar year exceeds $100. Cf. Model Code of Jud. Conduct rs. 3.14(A), 3.15(A)(3) (Am. Bar Ass'n 2011) (requiring the reporting of expense reimbursements and fee waivers from "sources other than the judge's employing entity," when the individual or combined amount received from the same source in a calendar year exceeds a specified amount). The Canon 6A(3) reporting requirement is similar to the reporting requirement for expense reimbursements and waivers in Rule 3.15(A)(3) of the American Bar Association Model Code of Judicial Conduct (2011), in that reimbursements, payments, and waivers must be reported if the amount of reimbursement, payment, or waiver, alone or in the aggregate with other reimbursements, payments, or waivers received from the same source in the same calendar year, exceeds the specified amount of $100. However, unlike the model rule, the amount of a reportable reimbursement, payment, or waiver does not have to be reported on Form 6A. Unlike gifts, the amount of which must be reported on that form, only the dates, location, and purpose of the event or activity for which expenses, fees, or charges were reimbursed, paid, or waived must be reported.

Canons 6B and 6C. Subparagraph A prescribes guidelines for additional compensation, reimbursements, or direct payments of expenses, and waivers of fees or charges accepted by a judge. Subparagraphs B and C prescribe the three types of financial disclosure reports required of each judicial officer.The filing of the disclosure reports required under Canon 6B is the only public disclosure of financial interests, compensation, gifts, expense reimbursements, or other benefits that a judge is required to make under this Code or the Florida Constitution. By filing the required disclosure reports, a judge fulfills all the expectations of conduct, and ethical and constitutional requirements related to such disclosure.

The first disclosure report is the Ethics Commission's constitutionally required form pursuant to Article II,

Section 8, of the Constitution. It must be filed each year as prescribed by law. The financial reporting period is for the previous calendar year. A final disclosure statement generally is required when a judge leaves office. The filing of the income tax return is a permissible alternative.

The second is a report of gifts, reimbursements or direct payments of expenses, and waivers of fees or charges accepted during the preceding calendar year to be filed publicly with the Florida Commission on Ethics. The gifts to be reported are in accordance with Canons 5D(5)(a) and 5D(5)(h). The expense reimbursements and payments, and waivers to be reported are in accordance with Canon 6A(3). This reporting is in lieu of that prescribed by statute as stated in the Supreme Court's opinion rendered inIn re Code of Judicial Conduct, 281 So. 2d 21 (Fla. 1973) . The form for this report is as follows:

Form 6A. Disclosure of Gifts, Expense Reimbursements or Payments, and Waivers of Fees and Charges

All judicial officers must file with the Florida Commission on Ethics a list of all reportable gifts accepted, and reimbursements or direct payments of expenses, and waivers of fees or charges accepted from sources other than the state or a judicial branch entity as defined in Florida Rule of Judicial Administration 2.420(b)(2), during the preceding calendar year as provided in Canons 5D(5)(a) and 5D(5)(h), Canon 6A(3), and Canon 6B(2) of the Code of Judicial Conduct, by date received, description (including dates, location, and purpose of event or activity for which expenses, fees, or charges were reimbursed, paid, or waived), source's name, and amount for gifts only.

Name: Work Telephone: Work Address: Judicial Office Held:

1. Please identify all reportable gifts you received during the preceding calendar year, as required by Canons 5D(5)(a), 5D(5)(h), and 6B(2) of the Code of Judicial Conduct.

DATE

DESCRIPTION

SOURCE

AMOUNT

Check here if continued on separate sheet

2. Please identify all reportable reimbursements or direct payments of expenses, and waivers of fees or charges you received during the preceding calendar year, as required by Canons 6A(3) and 6B(2) of the Code of Judicial

Conduct.

DATE

DESCRIPTION (Include dates, location, and purpose of event or activity for which expenses, fees, or charges were reimbursed, paid, or waived)

SOURCE

Check here if continued on separate sheet

OATH
State of Florida
County of
I, , the public official filing this disclosure statement, being first duly sworn, do depose on oath and say that the facts set forth in the above statement are true, correct, and complete to the best of my knowledge and belief.

(Signature of Reporting Official)

(Signature of Officer Authorized to Administer Oaths)

My Commission expires .

Sworn to and subscribed before me this day of 20 .

COMMENTARY [cont'd]
The third financial disclosure report is prescribed in subparagraph C. This provision ensures that there will

be complete financial information for all judicial officers available with the Judicial Qualifications Commission by requiring that full disclosure be filed confidentially with the Judicial Qualifications Commission in the event the limited disclosure alternative is selected under the provisions of Article II, Section 8.

The amendment to this Canon requires in 6B(2) a separate gift report to be filed with the Florida Commission on Ethics on or before July 1 of each year. The form to be used for that report is included in the commentary to Canon 6. It should be noted that Canon 5, as it presently exists, restricts and prohibits the acceptance of certain gifts. This provision is not applicable to other public officials.

With reference to financial disclosure if the judge chooses the limited disclosure alternative available under the provision of Article II, Section 8, of the Constitution of Florida, without the inclusion of the judge's Federal Income Tax Return, then the judge must file with the Commission a list of the names of corporations or other business entities in which the judge has a financial interest even though the amount is less than $1,000. This information remains confidential until a request is made by a party to a cause before the judge. This latter provision continues to ensure that complete financial information for all judicial officers is available with the Judicial Qualifications Commission and that parties who are concerned about a judge's possible financial interest have a means of obtaining that information as it pertains to a particular cause before the judge.

Canon 6D. Section 3E requires a judge to disqualify himself or herself in any proceeding in which the judge has an economic interest. See "economic interest" as explained in the Definitions Section. Canon 5D requires a judge to refrain from engaging in business and from financial activities that might interfere with the impartial performance of judicial duties; Section 6B requires a judge to report all compensation the judge received for activities outside judicial office. A judge has the rights of any other citizen, including the right to privacy of the judge's financial affairs, except to the extent that limitations established by law are required to safeguard the proper performance of the judge's duties.

[Commentary amended Jan. 10, 2002 (816 So. 2d 1084); May 18, 2017 effective Jan. 1, 2017 (218 So. 3d 432); May 10, 2018 (242 So. 3d 319).]

Canon 7

A Judge or Candidate for Judicial Office Shall Refrain from Inappropriate Political Activity

An Aid to Understanding Canon 7 (updated October 2018) - Download this free booklet explaining the ethical restrictions that apply to candidates in judicial elections. https://www.flcourts.org/content/download/218065/1974336/canon7.pdf

A. All judges and Candidates.

(1) Except as authorized in Sections 7B(2), 7C(2) and 7C(3), a judge or a candidate for election or appointment to judicial office shall not:

(a) act as a leader or hold an office in a political organization;

(b) publicly endorse or publicly oppose another candidate for public office;

(c) make speeches on behalf of a political organization;

(d) attend political party functions; or

(e) solicit funds for, pay an assessment to or make a contribution to a political organization or candidate, or purchase tickets for political party dinners or other functions.

(2) A judge shall resign from judicial office upon becoming a candidate for a non-judicial office either in a primary or in a general election, except that the judge may continue to hold judicial office while being a candidate for election to or serving as a delegate in a state constitutional convention if the judge is otherwise permitted by law to do so.

(3) A candidate for a judicial office:

(a) shall be faithful to the law and maintain professional competence in it, and shall not be swayed by partisan interests, public clamor, or fear of criticism;

(b) shall maintain the dignity appropriate to judicial office and act in a manner consistent with the impartiality, integrity, and independence of the judiciary, and shall encourage members of the candidate's family to adhere to the same standards of political conduct in support of the candidate as apply to the candidate;

(c) shall prohibit employees and officials who serve at the pleasure of the candidate, and shall discourage other employees and officials subject to the candidate's direction and control from doing on the candidate's behalf what the candidate is prohibited from doing under the Sections of this Canon;

(d) except to the extent permitted by Section 7C(1),

shall not authorize or knowingly permit any other person to do for the candidate what the candidate is prohibited from doing under the Sections of this Canon;

(e) shall not:

(i) with respect to parties or classes of parties, cases, controversies, or issues that are likely to come before the court, make pledges, promises, or commitments that are inconsistent with the impartial performance of the adjudicative duties of the office; or

(ii) knowingly misrepresent the identity, qualifications, present position or other fact concerning the candidate or an opponent;

(iii) while a proceeding is pending or impending in any court, make any public comment that might reasonably be expected to affect its outcome or impair its fairness or make any nonpublic comment that might substantially interfere with a fair trial or hearing. This section does not apply to proceedings in which the judicial candidate is a litigant in a personal capacity.

(iv) commend or criticize jurors for their verdict, other than in a court pleading, filing, or hearing in which the candidate represents a party in the proceeding in which the verdict was rendered.

(f) may respond to personal attacks or attacks on the

candidate's record as long as the response does not violate Section 7A(3)(e).

B. Candidates Seeking Appointment to Judicial or Other Governmental Office.

(1) A candidate for appointment to judicial office or a judge seeking other governmental office shall not solicit or accept funds, personally or through a committee or otherwise, to support his or her candidacy.

(2) A candidate for appointment to judicial office or a judge seeking other governmental office shall not engage in any political activity to secure the appointment except that:

(a) such persons may:

(i) communicate with the appointing authority, including any selection or nominating commission or other agency designated to screen candidates;

(ii) seek support or endorsement for the appointment from organizations that regularly make recommendations for reappointment or appointment to the office, and from individuals; and

(iii) provide to those specified in Sections 7B(2)(a)(i) and 7B(2)(a)(ii) information as to his or her qualifications for the office;

(b) a non-judge candidate for appointment to judicial office may, in addition, unless otherwise prohibited by law:

(i) retain an office in a political organization,

(ii) attend political gatherings, and

(iii) continue to pay ordinary assessments and ordinary contributions to a political organization or candidate and purchase tickets for political party dinners or other functions.

C. Judges and Candidates Subject to Public Election.

(1) A candidate, including an incumbent judge, for a judicial office that is filled by public election between competing candidates shall not personally solicit campaign funds, or solicit attorneys for publicly stated support, but may establish committees of responsible persons to secure and manage the expenditure of funds for the candidate's campaign and to obtain public statements of support for his or her candidacy. Such committees are not prohibited from soliciting campaign contributions and public support from any person or corporation authorized by law. A candidate shall not use or permit the use of campaign contributions for the private benefit of the candidate or members of the candidate's family.

(2) A candidate for merit retention in office may conduct only limited campaign activities until such time as the judge certifies that the judge's candidacy has drawn active opposition. Limited campaign activities shall only include the conduct authorized by subsection C(1), interviews with reporters and editors of the print, audio and visual media, and appearances and speaking engagements before public gatherings and organizations. Upon mailing a certificate in writing to the Secretary of State, Division of Elections, with a copy to the Judicial Qualifications Commission, that the judge's candidacy has drawn active opposition, and specifying the nature thereof, a judge may thereafter campaign in any manner authorized by law, subject to the restrictions of subsection A(3). This includes candidates facing active opposition in a merit retention election for the same judicial office campaigning together and conducting a joint campaign designed to educate the public on merit retention and each candidate's views as to why he or she should be retained in office, to the extent not otherwise prohibited by Florida law.

(3) A judicial candidate involved in an election or re-election, or a merit retention candidate who has certified that he or she has active opposition, may attend a political party function to speak in behalf of his or her candidacy or on a matter that relates to the law, the

improvement of the legal system, or the administration of justice. The function must not be a fund raiser, and the invitation to speak must also include the other candidates, if any, for that office. The candidate should refrain from commenting on the candidate's affiliation with any political party or other candidate, and should avoid expressing a position on any political issue. A judicial candidate attending a political party function must avoid conduct that suggests or appears to suggest support of or opposition to a political party, a political issue, or another candidate. Conduct limited to that described above does not constitute participation in a partisan political party activity.

D. Incumbent Judges. A judge shall not engage in any political activity except (i) as authorized under any other Section of this Code, (ii) on behalf of measures to improve the law, the legal system or the administration of justice, or (iii) as expressly authorized by law.

E. Applicability. Canon 7 generally applies to all incumbent judges and judicial candidates. A successful candidate, whether or not an incumbent, is subject to judicial discipline for his or her campaign conduct; an unsuccessful candidate who is a lawyer is subject to lawyer discipline for his or her campaign conduct. A lawyer who is a candidate for judicial office is subject to

Rule 4-8.2(b) of the Rules Regulating The Florida Bar.

F. Statement of Candidate for Judicial Office. Each candidate for a judicial office, including an incumbent judge, shall file a statement with the qualifying officer within 10 days after filing the appointment of campaign treasurer and designation of campaign depository, stating that the candidate has read and understands the requirements of the Florida Code of Judicial Conduct. Such statement shall be in substantially the following form:

STATEMENT OF CANDIDATE FOR JUDICIAL OFFICE

I, , the judicial candidate, have received, have read, and understand the requirements of the Florida Code of Judicial Conduct.

Signature of Candidate

Date

COMMENTARY

Canon 7A(1). A judge or candidate for judicial office retains the right to participate in the political process as a voter.

Where false information concerning a judicial candidate is made public, a judge or another judicial candidate having knowledge of the facts is not prohibited by Section 7A(1) from making the facts public.

Section 7A(1)(a) does not prohibit a candidate for elective judicial office from retaining during candidacy a public office such as county prosecutor, which is not "an office in a political organization."

Section 7A(1)(b) does not prohibit a judge or judicial candidate from privately expressing his or her views on judicial candidates or other candidates for public office.

A candidate does not publicly endorse another candidate for public office by having that candidate's name on the same ticket.

Section 7A(1)(b) prohibits judges and judicial candidates from publicly endorsing or opposing candidates for public office to prevent them from abusing the prestige of judicial office to advance the interests of others. Section 7C(2) authorizes candidates facing active opposition in a merit retention election for the same judicial office to campaign together and conduct a joint campaign designed to educate the public on merit retention and each candidate's views as to why he or she should be retained in office, to the extent not otherwise prohibited by Florida law. Joint campaigning by merit retention candidates, as authorized under Section 7C(2), is not a prohibited public endorsement of another candidate under Section 7A(1)(b).

Canon 7A(3)(b). Although a judicial candidate must encourage members of his or her family to adhere to the same standards of political conduct in support of the candidate that apply to the candidate, family members are free to participate in other political activity.

Canon 7A(3)(e). Section 7A(3)(e) prohibits a candidate for judicial office from making statements that commit the candidate regarding cases, controversies or issues likely to come before the court. As a corollary, a candidate should emphasize in any public statement the candidate's duty to uphold the law regardless of his or her personal views. Section 7A(3)(e) does not prohibit a candidate from making pledges or promises respecting improvements in court administration. Nor does this Section prohibit an incumbent judge from making private statements to other judges or court personnel in the performance of judicial duties. This Section applies to any statement made in the process of securing judicial office, such as statements to commissions charged with judicial selection and tenure and legislative bodies confirming appointment.

Canon 7B(2). Section 7B(2) provides a limited exception to the restrictions imposed by Sections 7A(1) and 7D.

Under Section 7B(2), candidates seeking reappointment to the same judicial office or appointment to another judicial office or other governmental office may apply for the appointment and seek appropriate support.

Although under Section 7B(2) non-judge candidates seeking appointment to judicial office are permitted during candidacy to retain office in a political organization, attend political gatherings and pay ordinary dues and assessments, they remain subject to other provisions of this Code during candidacy. See Sections 7B(1), 7B(2)(a), 7E and Application Section.

Canon 7C. The term "limited campaign activities" is not intended to permit the use of common forms of campaign advertisement which include, but are not limited to, billboards, bumperstickers, media commercials, newspaper advertisements, signs, etc. Informational brochures about the merit retention system, the law, the legal system or the administration of justice, and neutral, factual biographical sketches of the candidates do not violate this provision.

Active opposition is difficult to define but is intended to include any form of organized public opposition or an unfavorable vote on a bar poll. Any political activity engaged in by members of a judge's family should be conducted in the name of the individual family member, entirely independent of the judge and without reference to the judge or to the judge's office.

Canon 7D. Neither Section 7D nor any other section of the Code prohibits a judge in the exercise of administrative functions from engaging in planning and other official activities with members of the executive and legislative branches of government. With respect to a judge's activity on behalf of measures to improve the law, the legal system and the administration of justice, see Commentary to Section 4B and Section 4C and its Commentary.

Application and Commentary

Revised 05/21/2021

This Code applies to justices of the Supreme Court and judges of the District Courts of Appeal, Circuit Courts, and County Courts.

Anyone, whether or not a lawyer, who performs judicial functions, including but not limited to a civil traffic infraction hearing officer, court commissioner, general or special magistrate, domestic relations commissioner, child support hearing officer, or judge of compensation claims, shall, while performing judicial functions, conform with Canons 1, 2A, and 3, and such other provisions of this

Code that might reasonably be applicable depending on the nature of the judicial function performed.

Any judge responsible for a person who performs a judicial function should require compliance with the applicable provisions of this Code.

If the hiring or appointing authority for persons who perform a judicial function is not a judge then that authority should adopt the applicable provisions of this Code.

A. Civil Traffic Infraction Hearing Officer

A civil traffic infraction hearing officer: (1) is not required to comply with Sections 5C(2), 5D(2) and (3), 5E, 5F, and 5G, and Sections 6B and 6C. (2) should not practice law in the civil or criminal traffic court in any county in which the civil traffic infraction hearing officer presides.

B. Retired/Senior Judge

(1) A retired judge eligible to serve on assignment to temporary judicial duty, hereinafter referred to as "senior judge," shall comply with all the provisions of this Code except Sections 5C(2), 5E, 5F(1), and 6A. A senior judge shall not practice law or serve as a mediator, arbitrator, or voluntary trial resolution judge in a circuit in which the judge is presiding over civil cases as a senior judge,

and shall refrain from accepting any assignment in any cause in which the judge's present financial business dealings, investments, or other extra-judicial activities might be directly or indirectly affected.

(2) If a retired justice or judge does not desire to be assigned to judicial service, such justice or judge who is a member of The Florida Bar may engage in the practice of law and still be entitled to receive retirement compensation. The justice or judge shall then be entitled to all the rights of an attorney-at-law and no longer be subject to this Code.

COMMENTARY

Section A. Please see *In re Florida Rules of Practice and Procedure for Traffic Courts–Civil Traffic Infraction Hearing Officer Pilot Program*, 559 So.2d 1101 (Fla.1990), regarding civil traffic infraction hearing officers.

Amendments and Notes

Effective Date of Compliance

A person to whom this Code becomes applicable shall comply immediately with all provisions of this Code except Sections 5D(2), 5D(3) and 5E and shall comply with these Sections as soon as reasonably possible and shall do so in any event within the period of one year.

COMMENTARY

If serving as a fiduciary when selected as judge, a new judge may, notwithstanding the prohibitions in Section 5E, continue to serve as fiduciary but only for that period of time necessary to avoid serious adverse consequences to the beneficiary of the fiduciary relationship and in no event longer than one year. Similarly, if engaged at the time of judicial selection in a business activity, a new judge may, notwithstanding the prohibitions in Section 5D(3), continue in that activity for a reasonable period but in no event longer than one year.

www.ingramcontent.com/pod-product-compliance
Lightning Source LLC
LaVergne TN
LVHW052259200926
848481LV00002B/408